WE ALL DREAM OF A TEAM OF

CARRAGHERS

TRIBUTE TO A LIVERPOOL LEGEND

This Is Anfield
www.thisisanfield.com

First published worldwide by This Is Anfield, 2013

Text copyright © Matt Ladson, Max Munton, John Ritchie, Dan Holland, Matt Sproston, Dave Usher, Gavin Cooney, 2013

ISBN 978 1484 99266 1

Contents

Foreword

When the full-time whistle blew to signal the end of the final game of the 2012/13 season, as Liverpool beat Queens Park Rangers 1-0 at Anfield, it brought down the curtain on the career of Jamie Carragher's sixteen years as a Liverpool player.

737 appearances, 11 trophy successes and hundreds of abiding memories were consigned to history as one of the club's greatest servants hung up his boots. As Carragher walked around the famous stadium to rapturous applause and the sound of 'We all dream of a team of Carraghers' being sung from The Kop, supporters were saying thanks to the club's second highest ever appearance holder and a man who showed that determination, drive and desire can create incredible results.

For many who have grown up in the Premier League era the 2013/14 season will be the first time the name of Jamie Carragher won't be listed in the Liverpool squad. Carragher's retirement, coming when he had started 15 of the last 16 Liverpool matches, could perhaps have been seen as somewhat premature. But take a look at his interview with Sky Sports prior to his final Merseyside derby appearance to understand why he is doing it now - "I didn't want it to end with me in my suit up in the director's box". That quote personifies his footballing career. He is and was an old-fashioned footballer; not a modern day footballer seeking the fame and riches that the modern game brings, but a proper footballer who wanted to play every minute of every match.

Inside this special tribute to the one-club man we bring you contributions from a host of the writers at This Is Anfield, as well taking a look back through Jamie's career, bringing you all the best quotes, stats and memories in the process.

You'll find a superb piece from Matt Sproston taking a look at where Carragher ranks among the club's greatest centre-halves; Dan Holland ponders what's next for Carra after retirement and shares his hopes for him to remain involved at LFC; Gavin Cooney writes a personal tribute; while John Ritchie reminisces about *that* night in Istanbul.

We're also delighted that Dave Usher from The Liverpool Way fanzine has allowed us to publish an interview he conducted with the man himself shortly after the 2005 Champions League success. In it, Carra talks about that famous night, Dudek's wobbly legs, and puts the record straight on the Everton tattoo rumours!

Thanks for reading and we hope you enjoy the book as much as we have enjoyed taking a look back at the career of one of Anfield's true greats and a real role model for your children and grand-children.

Matt and Max
Editors, thisisanfield.com

Timeline

1987 - Joins Liverpool academy as 9 year-old

1996 - Part of the famous FA Youth Cup winning team featuring Michael Owen

1996 - Turns professional

1997 - Makes his Liverpool debut against Middlesbrough in the League Cup 5th Round

1997 - Scores his first goal for the club on his full debut against Aston Villa

1999 - Makes England debut against Hungary

2000 - Breaks the England Under 21 appearance record with 27 caps

2001 - Collects first trophy as a Liverpool player - scoring in the penalty shoot-out in the League Cup Final to defeat Birmingham at the Millennium Stadium

2001 - Follows up the League Cup with FA Cup, UEFA Cup, Charity Shield and European Super Cup success

2003 - Ruled out for 6 months with a broken leg after a foul by Blackburn's Lucas Neill

2005 - Wins European Cup in Istanbul

2005 - Named Liverpool Player of the Year

2006 - Named in the PFA Team of the Year

2006 - Part of the England squad for the World Cup

2007 - Runner up in the Champions League Final, losing out to AC Milan in Athens

2007 - Named Liverpool Player of the Year for a second time

2008 - Given a guard of honour as he makes his 500th appearance for the club against Luton in the FA Cup

2009 - Launches The 23 Foundation charity

2010 - Plays his last game for England, against Algeria in World Cup, South Africa

2011 - Testimonial against Everton, raising £1m for charity

2013 - Announces his retirement from football at the end of the season

2013 - Confirmed that Carragher will join Sky Sports as a pundit after retirement

2013 - Plays his final game for Liverpool against QPR, at Anfield

Carra by Numbers

26 - years at Liverpool FC

737 - appearances

1 - European Cup

2 - FA Cups

3 - League Cups

12 - honours with LFC (incl. Youth Cup)

5 - goals scored

150 - appearances in Europe for Liverpool FC

23 - shirt number throughout his career

2 - times Liverpool Player of the Season (2005, 2007)

1 - club

History will not leave Carragher in the shadows

by Gavin Cooney

The dictionary definition of 'soccer' is boring. For those interested, here it is:

> 'a form of football played between two teams of 11 players, in which the ball may be advanced by kicking or bouncing it off any part of the body but the arms and hands, except in the case of the goalkeepers, who may use their hands to catch, carry, throw or stop the ball'

See what I meant by boring?

Needless to say, it's also incomplete. There wouldn't be enough space in any dictionary to describe what football means to us all. If there was even an attempt to do so, other uncommon words would have to be cut in the interests of pragmatism. Abrogation? You're gone. Abnegate? Give up your place, will you? Ephemeral? You're not lasting long. Obstreperous? Please go without a fight. Football means an awful lot of things to an awful lot of people. It's most powerful feature however, is its capacity to represent. Football is defined by culture, and culture is defined by football. The tiki-taka of Spain is similar to the cruel baiting of the bull – fighting rings. The almost gratuitous flicks and tricks of diminutive Brazilians is a symbol of the kid on the street's wily ability to beat the system. Managers prepare teams to exploit the fluidity of the game in such ways as to define themselves. The players wear crests of town, city, and country. The fans wave flags, make banners and sing songs, identifying themselves with their home place. Football defines a culture. It is a bicep-bulging bulwark of self-expression, self-defence and self-esteem. We love football because it speaks us. It amplifies our thoughts, feelings, emotions and beliefs through goals, tackles, tricks, determination. The eleven men on the pitch represent the thousands in the stands. How do we fit all of that in a dictionary? For the people of Liverpool there is a way. It needs only two words. Jamie Carragher.

The name stirs the mind. Hunched over, hands on knees. Back straight, arms gesticulating, bellowing instructions. Talking. Always talking. Fists clenched. Leg outstretched. Arms aloft. A smile as wide as the Mersey. These are some of the images of Carragher that come to Scouse minds when his name is mentioned. The most common compliment paid to the boy from Bootle is that he is one of us. If he wasn't roaring at teammates to get in position, he would be directing them from the Kop. His passion, intensity, commitment and spirit reflect what those pay to see him ooze from their pores. While it is a worthy compliment, it is not wholly satisfying. Pick anyone off the Kop on a Saturday afternoon, and with shorts and shin pads, they would run around and work hard for ninety minutes.* It is, however, unlikely that they would be called back the following Saturday, let alone for another 700 Saturdays after that. It may sound like a staggering understatement, but Jamie Carragher was a bloody good footballer. While lacking pace, occasionally finesse and not exactly prolific in front of the opposition goal, Anfield has rarely seen a better reader of the game. Had Carragher penned 'Football 101', Arrigo Sacchi would have read it. And recommended it to Johan Cruyff.

Of course, it wasn't just Anfield that saw Carragher's innate and astounding abilities. Old Trafford, Stamford Bridge, Goodison Park, Camp Nou, The Bernabeu, and the San Siro were the many football cauldrons that witnessed Carragher's irresistible blend of focus, raw passion and coolness under pressure. Liverpool are a footballing institution, and as a result their greatest players must test themselves on the greatest stages. Carragher was handed his lines on the European stage, and he delivered them with aplomb. His integral part in rebuilding Anfield as a European fortress is, in my opinion, his greatest legacy. He, along with Steven Gerrard, led their home club into the most daunting footballing cauldrons in the world, and conquered them.

Here, we return to football's greatest characteristic: the power of representation. Carragher, with a liverbird on his chest, epitomised that. Liverpool was the city that Thatcher hated, the working class city that didn't fit with London's political elite. Liverpool was the city which was slandered, abused, laughed at. But it never lay down. This relatively small city in the North-West of the country stood firm, and partly through football, built a reputation in the face of adversity. It became the capital of football, as the league title's journey was often restricted to a short trip across Stanley Park. As the decades passed, the city's reputation grew. From riots in Toxteth to European Capital of Culture in 2008. In the mid to late 2000s, Liverpool Football Club reminded the world just what it meant to be to be from Liverpool. They did so with a Spanish manager, but a Scouse heart. And that pumping heart was Jamie Carragher. Watching him shackle the greatest players the world produced of the time was life – affirming. Eto'o, Shevchenko, Crespo (okay, aside for forty-five minutes), Ibrahimovic, Messi, Drogba. It was glorious. Liverpool fans were often shoved into small corners in the skies of footballing cathedrals across Europe, but one of them was on the pitch, in the heat of battle. Liverpool Football Club regained credibility with the many European conquests that Rafa Benitez assembled. Jamie Carragher was one of his chief orchestrators. Not least on one night in Istanbul.

That night, watching Liverpool and Carragher was an extraordinary fusion of pain and ecstasy. The first half was unrelentingly miserable, an incredibly talented Milan team tore Liverpool to shreds for forty- five minutes. There was the pain. Then, the most stunning of comebacks. Ecstasy. From then on, Scouse emotions swung uncontrollably between both. The realisation that we were going to leave the goals scored at just the three. That momentary horror when we realised that, were we to win, it would mean the greatest rear-guard action we had ever seen. Then the rallying call, as we collectively started into the fiery abyss of an onslaught from one of the finest teams in the world. Everyone has their outstanding memories from that game. Mine is, and forever will be, Jamie Carragher's anguishing efforts to stop Milan from scoring. Carragher, as well as all the Liverpool players from the sixty-first minute onwards, stood tall in the face of a storm. The images of Carragher lying on the turf, screaming in pain from chronic cramp, but then picking himself up to push himself even further have entered that hallowed album entitled 'Liverpool FC in Europe'. The pain was blatantly debilitating, but Carragher realised he was playing for something eternal. Glory.

I can say wholeheartedly, as a supporter, it was an honour to see Jamie Carragher play that night in Istanbul. But then, it has been an honour for more than a decade. It was an honour to see him keep a clean sheet. It was an honour to see him win a tackle. It was an honour to see him haul down Joleon Lescott in the penalty area, act like nothing untoward happened, and then race to the Liverpool fans at Goodison in jubilation at the final whistle. It was an honour to see him outmuscle Zlatan Ibrahimovic. It was an honour to see him dispossess Didier Drogba. It was an honour to see him attempt to soldier on after breaking his leg. It was an honour to see him win a game. It was an honour to see him win trophies. It was an honour to see one of us in a Liverpool shirt week in, week out. It was an honour to have Jamie Carragher represent my club.

There is one more image of Jamie that clings to my mind. Having toed the Rubicon of physical limitations in Istanbul , the cramp returned on the podium. Just as Steven Gerrard lifted the European Cup, Carragher was left hunched, in pain, in the shadows. Josemi took his rightful place alongside the captain. While Carragher was left in the shadows then, history won't leave him there. Jamie Carragher retires as a Liverpool legend. Thank you   Jamie,   it's   been   an   honour.

The Early Years - Bootle Boy Arrives on Kop

by Matt Ladson

James Lee Duncan Carragher was born in Alder Hey Children's Hospital in West Derby, Liverpool on 28th January 1978, where he remained in hospital for the first six weeks of his life due to gastroschisis -- perhaps that was the first sign of his fighting spirit that would go on to become a trademark of his sixteen year career as a Liverpool FC player.

He attended St. James' Primary School in his hometown of Bootle on Merseyside and began playing football for his school aged 8. He soon signed for Brunswick Boys' Club where he played 5-a-side most nights, and represented Merton Villa Under 11's. At age 9 he was already making strides in grassroots football, representing his district playing for Bootle Boys Under 11's. By age 10 he was captaining the side.

Carragher grew up as a huge Everton supporter; "I was a total Everton fanatic right through my childhood and teens," he confessed in an interview in 2008. "Everton controlled my life and dominated my thoughts 24/7. I went to the away games, followed them across Europe and in the mid-80s went to Wembley so often it began to feel like Alton Towers."

"It has been too long since Liverpool won the title - the last time they did, I was an Everton fan" he once joked.

Carragher grew up on Knowsley Road in Bootle, where he lived with his parents Paula and Phil and two brothers John and Paul. As a teenager, Carragher attended the former FA School of Excellence at Lilleshall, before signing as a youth team scholar (YTS) with Liverpool at the age of 16.

Carragher was part of the FA Youth Cup winning side of 1996, where 20,000 spectators attended the second-leg of the Final at Anfield as Michael Owen scored one of the goals on the night against a West Ham side featuring Rio Ferdinand and Frank Lampard.

That summer Carragher inherited the number 23 shirt, formerly worn by another academy graduate who was taking the Premier League by storm - a certain Robbie Fowler.

It was Roy Evans, in his penultimate full season as sole manager, who gave the soon-to-be 19-year-old his first-team debut in January 1997, coming on as a substitute for Rob Jones in a League Cup tie at Middlesbrough. It was a debut that had been expected for a while because Carragher's presence had been carefully monitored through his days at Lilleshall and as a member of Liverpool's Youth Cup team.

3 days later Carragher replaced Neil Ruddock at half-time in a 0-0 draw with West Ham at Anfield and a week later Jamie was handed his first start for the club, against Aston Villa on January 18th 1997. Such an occasion was marked in fine style by heading in a left-wing corner in front of the Kop to set his team on the way to a comfortable 3-0 victory. Goals for Liverpool have come rarely for Carragher and this was one of the highlights of his career: "I knew the night before, I was down to play at centre-half but Bjørn Kvarme's clearance came through before 5 pm that night but I didn't realise. I wouldn't have been playing only that Patrik Berger was sick that night, so there was a place and I was moved into midfield. I was a bit nervous, but it was more excitement really. I got booked after 20 seconds, that calmed me down."

That proved to be his only start of the season as Liverpool sought to challenge Man United for the title. Carragher was named on the bench for five games, including the second leg of the European Cup Winners Cup semi-final against Paris St. Germain. Ultimately Evans' side ended the season without any silverware but there was much hope for the future in the shape of Carragher and fellow academy team-mate and friend Michel Owen, who made his debut with two games remaining at Wimbledon.

The following season, 1997-98, saw Carragher make 20 starts - the first being another 3-0 win over Aston Villa at Anfield in September. He finished the season by starting in the last four consecutive games against West Ham, Chelsea, Arsenal and Derby County as Liverpool ended the season third, but 13 points behind Champions Arsenal.

That summer saw Liverpool appoint Gerard Houllier in joint-charge alongside Roy Evans and it was to prove a pivotal moment in Carragher's career. In an interview in 2010, Carragher explained "He was the biggest influence on my career because of what I won with him, how he influenced me as a player and what he gave me off the pitch."

Carragher entered the Liverpool team at the height of their 'Spice Boy' era and the Christmas party in 1998 was the incident that hit the headlines in the press as Carragher "got busy with a can of whipped cream and a gaggle of strippers while dressed as the Hunchback of Notre Dame" [The Mirror].

It was Houllier who provided some professional advice and after 500 games for the club, speaking in 2010 Carragher explained "It probably wouldn't have been possible [to play 650 games] without the advice he gave me off the pitch. He [Houllier] was the biggest influence on my career because of what I won with him, how he influenced me as a player and what he gave me off the pitch."

"If I did become a manager, of all the ones I've had, I'd probably be most similar in style to Gerard Houllier. He used to lose his temper a little bit - I think I'd lose mine as well."

Despite off the pitch controversy, Carragher became a key part of the side, starting 34 Premier League games and 44 in all competitions. It was a season of transition with the departure of

Roy Evans in November and Liverpool finished a lowly seventh - 25 points behind title winners Man United.

The 98/99 season was notable too for Carragher earning his first England cap, under manager Kevin Keegan, in a friendly against Hungary in April, replacing Rio Ferdinand for the last half an hour. He would go on to play in two World Cups and make 38 appearances for his country.

The Houllier Years

by Matt Sproston

Just as Jamie had established himself as a first team regular, his position within the starting line up came under threat. Gerard Houllier was in sole charge of the team following the abortive joint manager experiment and he set about rebuilding the team from the back.

Sami Hyypia and Stephane Henchoz were purchased in the summer of 1999 and would go on to form a centre back partnership that was the bedrock of Houllier's team. Didi Hamman was brought in to play in defensive midfield, another of Jamie's previous roles. This would be a recurring theme for the remainder of Houllier's management. As soon as Carra nailed down a position, a signing would be made to challenge him.

The 99-00 season would be a transitional one for the team as the many new signings settled in. Jamie was a reliable performer mainly at right back and contributed to the meanest defence in the Premier League. The only blot on Jamie's copybook would be a brace of own goals against Manchester United at Anfield in a 2-3 defeat early in the season. Despite that, Sami Hyypia was the only outfield player who made more starts than Jamie that season.

The team missed out on the Champions League qualifying places following a poor end to the season but did qualify for the UEFA Cup which would ultimately prove to be a blessing in disguise.

The 00-01 season was perhaps the most exciting in the club's history. Big game followed big game in a run in that upon reflection was scarcely believable. Carra was in the thick of it at the business end of the season having once again seen off more new signings intended to take his place in the starting line up.

This time Houllier bought German internationals Markus Babbel and Christian Ziege. Babbel was expected to play centre back but the magnificent form of Henchoz and Hyypia pushed him out to right back where Jamie had spent most of the previous season. Ziege started the season at left back but lacked the solidity that Houllier required and so once again Carra was back in the starting line up having to adapt to a new position.

From February onwards the team lost only 2 league games and of course were involved in 3 cup runs. Houllier rotated the team during the manic run in but essentially left the back four alone such was their magnificent form.

Carra picked up his first senior trophy as part of the team that won the Worthington Cup against Birmingham City in Cardiff. It was a largely forgettable game but memorable for the quality of Robbie Fowler's strike and for the quality of Carra's perfect penalty in the shootout.

The FA Cup run to the final was relatively straightforward but still included an away win against a fine Leeds United side. Carra took his place in the final team to face an Arsenal team who would go on to win the league the following season. Liverpool were outplayed for 80 minutes but, thanks to some last gasp defending, the deficit was kept to a single goal. Carra did his job keeping Robert Pires largely quiet. Michael Owen stepped up with 2 late goals to complete the smash and grab.

The UEFA Cup run was perhaps the most remarkable and also an indicator that Carra was now a serious player on the world stage. En route to the final, the Reds dispatched Olympiakos, Roma, Porto and Barcelona. Carra particularly excelled in away wins against Roma and Barcelona, both of whom were packed full of attacking talent.

The final against Alaves of Spain was the opposite to the games that had come before it. The Liverpool defence was woeful and what should have been a comfortable win became a crazy 5-4 scoreline and one of the most enjoyable European finals ever. Carra was running on empty and endured a torrid time against Alaves' attacking full back Cosmin Contra.

On top of the three trophies Liverpool secured Champions League qualification. It was quite a season and Carra himself would say that it was an even greater achievement than Istanbul.

2001-2002 saw Houllier splash out on specialist left back John Arne Riise. Again, Carra's place would be under threat and again he would rise to the challenge. Carra settled in at right back following Markus Babbel's illness. The team kicked on with the back four proving to be as reliable as ever despite the changing faces and positions. The league form was superb and there was real belief that the title could be won. However, Houllier's heart operation in October rocked the squad and although their form remained good, results around Christmas slipped and ultimately the Reds finished second.

Disappointment in both domestic cups included a red card for Jamie at Arsenal in the FA Cup. Arsenal fans threw a coin at Jamie and so he threw it back! A straight red card followed and an unreserved apology prevented any further charges although Jamie did receive a warning from the police.

The Reds fared better in the Champions League, reaching the quarter final stage beating Borussia Dortmund and Roma along the way. A poor performance away to Bayer Leverkusen cost the Reds a place in the semi finals and looking back was perhaps an early indication of Houllier's weakness following illness as he tinkered with the back four to accommodate Abel Xavier. Carra moved out to left back and the usually solid back four looked very vulnerable.

Another highlight of the season for Jamie was his involvement in England's 5-1 away win against Germany albeit as a substitute. However, a niggling knee injury required surgery and meant that he would miss the 2002 World Cup Finals.

2002-2003 was a step backwards for the club who trailed in fifth in the league despite a strong start to the season. Jamie did pick up another League Cup winners medal at the expense of Manchester United.

For the first time in years, no direct replacement was purchased for Jamie as Houllier threw his transfer kitty at El Hadji Diouf and Salif Diao. Jamie continued to be a solid performer mainly at right back but the consistency of the back four from previous years had started to diminish as Henchoz lost his place in the back four to Traore and Dudek lost his confidence. Houllier seemed unable to summon up the strength that had helped him to rebuild the club.

2003-2004 was perhaps Jamie's worst season at the club through no fault of his own. A horror tackle from Lucas Neill away to Blackburn in September broke Carra's leg. It would be four months before Jamie returned and it was a credit to him that he came back so quickly.

For the club, the season was a washout. Early exits from domestic and European cups meant that the season was effectively over in January. The Reds did qualify for the Champions League but it would not be Gerard Houllier who led them on the road to Istanbul.

Houllier's time was up and Benitez would replace him. Benitez would fine tune Carra as a defender and particularly as a centre half but it was Houllier that created Carra the professional. Jamie would later say that it was the right time for Houllier to be replaced but he always acknowledged the massive part Gerard Houllier played in his development turning him from a raw kid to a player on the world stage.

Rafa Arrives - Time for a Central Role

by Matt Ladson and Max Munton

When Gerard Houllier left Anfield in the summer of 2004, Spaniard Rafa Benitez was the man to replace him at the helm. After years of being a versatile squad player, Benitez moved Carragher permanently to centre-back, and alongside Sami Hyypia. The two of them forming a superb partnership and understanding. If the years prior to this season had left many pondering Carragher's best position - and indeed whether he could hold down a place in the first team at Anfield - this season answered all the questions. It was career defining.

Of course, the memories of Benitez's first season are defined by the images of Olympiakos, Juventus, Chelsea, and Istanbul. Carragher, Gerrard, Hyypia and Hamann were the key figures, with supporting roles from Garcia, Dudek, Alonso, Smicer and co. But beside from the Miracle of Istanbul, Carragher cemented himself as one of Europe's finest centre-backs. He started every Premier League game - a feat he would repeat again in the 2008/09 season - making a total of 56 appearances during an incredible season. Carra was voted the club's player of the season and later captained the side to UEFA Super Cup Success against CSKA Moscow in Monaco.

A year later and another trophy arrived in the Carragher cabinet; this time the FA Cup - won in almost as dramatic fashion, again 3-3 and again on penalties. West Ham were the opposition in Cardiff for what was incredibly Carragher's tenth final in 10 years. The day didn't start well for Jamie though, getting his feet muddled up and turning in Scanoli's cross to give the Hammers the lead after 20 minutes. Of course, the Reds came from 2-0 down and 3-2 in stoppage time before Pepe Reina played the part of Jerzy Dudek to make the crucial saves in the shoot-out.

Carragher then captained the side to Community Shield success before the 2006/07 season, lifting the trophy alongside Gerrard who came on as a second half sub. The match saw Benitez and Jose Mourinho go head-to-head once again and the Liverpool boss came out on top thanks to two superb goals from Riise and Crouch.

At the beginning of 2007, speculation mounted that a monumental sale of Liverpool Football Club would happen. David Moores sold his family's prize asset and two American businessmen completed the purchase of the club in February that year. Tom Hicks and George Gillett became the new co-chairmen of Liverpool, promising a bright future for the club, £200million investment in a new stadium, and picking up the club's £44.8million debt. More about how that turned out later.

The Americans joined the club at a positive time, taking giant steps forward on the pitch. The 2006/07 season saw Rafa Benitez's Liverpool finish seventh in the table and an emphatic Champions League campaign to reach their second European Cup Final under Benitez.

On route the Reds had overcome the likes of Barcelona, PSV Eindhoven and a dramatic semi-final penalty shoot-out against Chelsea. But it wasn't to be a repeat of 2005's heroics in Istanbul. A regimented, though somewhat aging, AC Milan side got revenge for the comeback two years earlier to lift their seventh European Cup title. Carragher, booked on the hour mark in the final, and Liverpool's defence, failed to deal with the attack of Italian striker Filippo Inzaghi. Inzaghi scored twice to sink the Reds, with only Dirk Kuyt's late header the reply at the Olympic Stadium in Athens.

Carragher published his story of his life and career so far in an autobiography titled 'Carra' in 2009. The book provides brilliant and intelligent anecdotes into his passion for the beautiful game. Carragher also revealed in the book his loyalty for club over country, remembering that when he missed a vital penalty for

England that saw them slump out of the 2006 World Cup in Germany to the hands of Portugal, he thought, 'Ah well, it's only England!'

Liverpool went on an almost triumphant run of form in the 2008/09 campaign, Carragher playing all 38 league games. Benitez led Liverpool to their best ever Premier League finish, second, behind Manchester United and an impressive points total of 86 points. The league campaign included a 4-1 victory over their arch rivals at Old Trafford, with Gerrard and Spanish striker Fernando Torres forming a formidable partnership.

In Europe, Carragher was a driving force too as Liverpool historically swept aside Spanish giants Real Madrid 5-0 on aggregate. At the time Carragher believed the blistering form of Gerrard and Torres would lead the Reds to their first league title since 1990. He said, "There is no better strike pairing in the world than Gerrard and Torres. They can tear defences wide open in a split second. When you have that kind of ability in your team it gives you incredible belief. If we can keep them both free of injury then we are going to take some stopping. There were times last year when we went into games without them and it showed."

In May 2009, our final away game of the season and our title challenge over after falling behind United, we saw an example of Carragher's undoubted passion and desire to win. 2-0 up against West Brom but with a clean-sheet to protect, Carragher's patience with full-back Alvaro Arbeloa had run out. The Spaniard had made one error too many and Carra let him know it, the pair having to be separated by Xabi Alonso. Afterwards, Carragher explained it was Pepe's clean-sheet record that made him so fired up: "We can't win the league now but there are a number of targets we can aim for. We wanted to keep a clean sheet and we want Pepe to have a chance of the Golden Glove for the third season running."

Despite continuing to be a permanent fixture in Liverpool's first team (37 league appearances in 2009/10), Carragher looked to a way to give something back to the community which had supported his career. He founded the '23 Foundation' with the slogan, 'Giving local kids a chance'. The organisation "aims to give local kids in Merseyside a chance to achieve their dreams through local charities, clubs and community initiatives by providing the means to make a difference." He said at the time, "I have really enjoyed my career to date at Liverpool Football Club and it is now time to do more and more for Charity in the Merseyside area. But how can I help? First of all along with my family and friends we decided to donate all the proceeds from my Testimonial year to Charity. Then after a great deal of consideration I decided that was not enough because I wanted to set up something that would last a lifetime and that is why the 23 Foundation was formed."

However, back at Anfield tension was mounting over Liverpool's spiraling debt problems brought about by Hicks and Gillett. Carragher recalled in an interview with the Liverpool Echo in 2011, "In the back of my mind I was thinking: this isn't right. One of them hasn't got the cash and the other doesn't really want to be here. This could end up going wrong." As fans demonstrations against the American owners intensified, a poor 2009/10 season, a real comedown from finishing second the 12 months before, cost Benitez his job.

Rafa was replaced by football journeyman Roy Hodgson, who had just enjoyed taking Fulham to the Europa League final and was the sweetheart of the British media. However, Hodgson's flirtation with life at Anfield would last just six months. Hodgson later became England manager and on Carragher announcing his retirement in 2013, backed the defender to become a great football coach: "After retirement I'm sure he will march quickly up the coaching ladder and become one of the country's top young coaches." Life under Hodgson saw the Reds plummet towards the relegation zone in the first half of the 2010/11 season, while a week of court battles in October 2010 saw an end to the days of Hicks and Gillett under messy circumstances.

Three members of Liverpool's board, Martin Broughton - a Chelsea supporting former British Airways chairman, Christian Purslow - a Harvard graduate who thought he could play Football Manager at Liverpool, and Scouser Ian Ayre, who would later become the club's Managing Director, took to the High Court to push a sale of the club to Boston based Fenway Sports Group against Hicks and Gillett's wishes. Carragher, along with most Reds fans, welcomed John Henry and FSG to Anfield with a degree of caution. He told press during that week of court battles, "Everyone knows it will be a good thing for the club. Hopefully it will be sorted sooner rather than later and we can start looking forward on the pitch and start improving results, which is what we need to do."

By Christmas in the 2010/11 season, Liverpool were at a new low. Embroiled in what was looking like it could be a horrible relegation battle after a poor start under Hodgson, the Reds went down 3-1 to Blackburn Rovers at Ewood Park on January 5th, 2011 - a game in which Carragher did not play a part of. Carragher was facing a fight for his place against Agger, Slovakian Martin Skrtel and Greek veteran Sotirios Kyrgiakos. He was also finding himself alongside the likes of not-so-inspiring Hodgson signings Paul Konchesky, Christian Poulsen and ex-Cheslea midfielder Joe Cole, a shadow of his former self.

Following that defeat at Blackburn, Hodgson was given his marching orders as the new owners put their foot down at Anfield. They brought in fans favourite and club legend Kenny Dalglish as caretaker boss to steady the ship. Amongst all this, Carragher was struggling with a dislocated shoulder, keeping him out of action for three months, yet he still made 28 league appearances - making a vital contribution to the first team - that season as Liverpool rose to finish a respectable sixth in the league.

By the 2011/12 season, Carragher was increasingly losing his place in the side, with critics pointing towards his aging pace. A strong partnership formed between Agger and Skrtel looked too good to break, but he still made 21 appearances during the league campaign and 10 more in successful domestic cup journeys.

What would be Carragher's final trophy with Liverpool was the 2012 League Cup, whern Dalglish's side defeated Cardiff City 3-2 on penalties after a 2-2 draw in the preceding 120 minutes. Carragher came off the bench in the 86th minute for Daniel Agger to partner Martin Skrtel for extra time. It was his first trip as a Reds player to Wembley Stadium since it was rebuilt and reopened in 2006. During the post-match celebrations, Carragher was quizzed by Sky Sports' Andy Burton as to whether the Cup success would be his swansong. He asked, "Just looking at you Jamie, you took some certain photos, and you're really soaking it up. You're not starting in the team at the moment – is this the start of a farewell?" To which a bemused Carragher replied, "No I don't think so. Who are you? The manager?!" before reminding Burton of his part in the recent Sky Sports sexism scandal.

Carragher and Liverpool returned to Wembley later that season as their FA Cup run took them all the way to the final. However, Carragher did not play a part in the 2-1 defeat to Chelsea and he and Liverpool walked away empty handed, finishing eighth in the league table as pressure mounted on Dalglish.

The Final Chapter - Renaissance under Rodgers

by Matt Ladson

When Brendan Rodgers was appointed successor to Kenny Dalglish ahead of the 2012/13 season, immediately lists were drawn up of players who would benefit from the Northern Irishman's arrival and his brand of 'tiki taka' style football. Carragher fell into the category who you thought wouldn't necessarily benefit, but as the season progressed he went from fourth choice to first choice centre back. An incredible and fitting renaissance in his final season ensued.

Early signs did not point to Carragher making 29 starts - 16 in the Premier League; beginning the season behind the first-choice partnership of Martin Skrtel and Daniel Agger, but also behind Sebastian Coates. The Uruguayan was picked ahead of Carragher for the first home game of the season, a 2-2 draw with newly crowned Champions Man City, and again was chosen for a key moment when Rodgers changed to three at the back in the Merseyside derby a few weeks later. Carragher was fourth choice of the four centre backs.

The difference in the two derbies show the turnaround in his - and Liverpool's - defence during the 2012/13 season. When the first derby of the season kicked off, at Goodison in late October, Jamie was yet to start a League game under Rodgers, with his only starts in the League and Europa Cup. With Coates chosen ahead of him, the derby was the fourth consecutive League game Carragher had sat on the bench watching on.

Perhaps this is when his mind was made up. In an interview with Sky Sports' Geoff Shreeves, shown before the home derby in May, Carragher explained "It's nice to finish being in the team. I didn't want to finish in the stand there being in the director's box with my suit on. And I thought that was how it's going to finish for me with being on the bench in the first half of the season and I didn't want it to end like that."

"I cant stand being a substitute."

"It doesn't matter what level of football you play at. When you're a kid and you see a gang of kids playing football in the park, if they said no you can't play you've got to watch from the side, it'd kill you wouldn't it."

Passion, sense and pride once again poured from Carragher's words.

But, between the away derby and the home derby in May - Carragher's thirtieth and final - things had changed. By now, Carragher had started 13 of the last 14 games in League and Cup - keeping six clean sheets in the process. That being since the FA Cup defeat at League One side Oldham. That match was the turning point in not only Carragher's season, but also Skrtel and Coates' - who had both started the match but were largely outmuscled by a player recently out of university football, Matt Smith. Rodgers was clearly furious "Matt Smith is a good player, but we have played against that type before." "If your application is not right, you can get found out."

Skrtel started just two matches between that Oldham defeat and the Merseyside derby - the away defeats to Zenit St. Petersburg and Southampton - while Coates never made a single minute. The only game Carragher missed, with a shin injury, was the disappointing defeat at Southampton. Afterwards Rodgers was asked if the side missed him "There's no question. For us, it's an area we feel we need to be better in."

Carragher had gone from fourth choice, peripheral squad member, to first-choice and the most important player in the side. Much of this was due to the player's attitude, application and desire - three characteristics Jamie had displayed throughout his career.

Jamie's final Merseyside derby ended in a dull affair, but at least a clean sheet was achieved, the match ending goalless. Reflecting on having made his final appearance against the side he grew up supporting, Carragher admitted "Yeah, it's sad because I love playing in those types of games but I'm just disappointed that we didn't get the result." Always focussed on the result. It meant that Carragher's derby record ended with 17 victories and just five defeats in 30 meetings between the two sides.

Soon after the derby, it was confirmed that Steven Gerrard would undergo shoulder surgery and therefore miss the final two games of the season at Fulham and at home to QPR - providing the perfect opportunity for Carragher to captain the side in his farewell appearances.

19th May, 2013, was the day Jamie Carragher's career took it's final bow - on a sunny day at Anfield. The Kop mosaic displayed 'JC 23', while the whole of Liverpool staff, along with visitors Queens Park Rangers, formed a guard of honour to salute Carra as he emerged from the Anfield tunnel one last time, alongside his daughter and son.

A solitary goal from Philippe Coutinho gave Liverpool victory, and the home side secured what was Carragher's 200th career clean sheet for the club. But it was almost capped in incredible fashion. Throughout the game the Anfield crowd had jokingly called for Carra to "shoooooottt" whenever he got the ball. On 62 minutes the ball fell invitingly, albeit 30 yards out, and Carragher took the opportunity - unleashing a half-volley that was struck perfectly. Sadly, it also struck the Kop goalpost with Robert Green comfortably beaten. "I think I would have just walked straight off if that had gone in" he joked afterwards. It would have been the perfect send-off - in the most unlikely fashion!

Carragher was replaced by Sebastian Coates in the 85th minute and with it his Liverpool career came to a close. Before taking a final lap of honour he spoke to the Anfield crowd:

"I'd just like to say to say thanks to everyone here today and to everyone who has supported me since I made my debut here in 1997."

"I've had lots of great times and memories. That's down to Liverpool Football Club and especially the fans. We've had some great nights here where the fans have dragged us over the line.

"I'd like to say thanks to all the supporters here today. Thank you."

Jamie, thank *you*.

From Utility Man to World Class Centre Half

by Dan Holland

In 16 memorable years, Jamie Carragher occupied a number of different positions for both club and country. But it was only under Rafa Benitez did he become a renowned centre half, revered across Europe as a no nonsense defender with impeccable timing in the tackle and unerring ability to read the game.

As a youth Jamie was, believe it or not, a centre forward for Bootle boys - in one season scoring 36 goals. Hard to believe isn't it of a man who in over 700 senior appearances has only scored 5 goals. He has even scored 8 goals *against* us - leaving him with an unenviable total of -3 goal difference. A minor blot on his otherwise exemplary career. We have, however, seen glimpses of his goalscoring ability including a goal on his full senior debut against Aston Villa at the Kop end and also the confidence to step up in penalty shoot outs in both domestic competitions and for England. Having said all that it was decided at a young age that Carra was not a Centre Forward.

In early 1997 Jamie made his first team debut in a League Cup Semi Final against Middlesbrough replacing Rob Jones in the 75th minute, his second appearance was also as substitute, this time replacing Neil Ruddock at half time. His full debut came on the 18th January, 1997, as a holding midfielder alongside Jamie Redknapp. In less than three weeks Carra had played right back, centre back and centre midfield, this short period typified his career for the first 7 years with left back added to the list of positions occupied by this at the time promising young player.

As a full back Carragher gave the defence an added security with his sound defensive qualities being superior to the other options available in each position. His added height was seen as an advantage at set pieces, the obvious limitations were his lack of pace and dribbling ability in an era were full backs were having more of an impact in the opposition half.

With each season that passed Carragher became a more important cog in the Liverpool wheel and would have perhaps cemented a more regular place in the heart of the Liverpool defence had it not been for the extremely successful partnership of Hyypia and Henchoz who filled these berths for the majority of games between 1999 and 2002. The natural side for Carra to have played would then have been Right Back but the impressive Markus Babbel occupied this role with aplomb for one season. So around the turn of the last century Carra was deployed as our first choice left back, the highest compliment I can pay him during this period is that I can't remember anybody outclassing him and at that time there were some pretty impressive right sided midfielders playing in the Premiership.

The following season saw another position change for Carra due to a combination of a debilitating illness that struck Babbel and the arrival of a superb left back in the shape of John Arne Riise. He was now back on his favoured right hand side albeit still in a full back role. His form was again imperious and not too many players came off the field getting the better of Mr Dependable.

Just prior to the arrival of a certain Rafael Benitez, Carra had started to inch out an ageing Stephane Henchoz and form an equally if not more impressive partnership with the big Finn, Sami Hyypia. In summary Carra's early years were influenced more by his fellow team mates than his undoubted ability. What I mean by that is he was chosen as left back ahead of players who considered this their specialist position until one was signed who was a better all-round full back which as I've previously mentioned is vital in todays game. Injury/illness to a player who was maybe a right back than him forced Houlliers hand and Jamie was trusted in that position again over other specialist right backs. A drop of form from Henchoz was the trigger that gave our No. 23 the role that he has now gone on to make his own and earn him the reputation which he rightly deserves.

Some may think that his early career could be summed up by the phrase 'jack of all trades, master of none'. For me this couldn't be more wrong, all his managers have had the utmost trust in him and considered him a 'master of all trades'.

Why did Jamie become such a good centre half who was loved across the Red half of Merseyside? I've already touched on his main attributes; his reading of the game and his ability to time a tackle but I think his impact goes far beyond this. In some ways Carra is unlucky to have played in the same era of Steven Gerrard because his goals and unerring ability to pick a pass stole all the headlines. But without Carra's organisation, his determination, his never say die attitude, his commitment, his bravery, his reluctance to accept anything less than 100% from his team mates and not to mention his match saving/winning goal line clearances, last ditch tackles and clearances. I doubt very much that we would have won that European Cup in Istanbul and countless other cup ties and league matches.

In 2007 I was lucky enough to be given the opportunity to present Carra with a Player of the Year trophy as voted for by the Grimsby Branch of the Liverpool Supporters Club. It was a brief meeting but what struck me was his humble and professional attitude, he certainly wasn't 'Mr Big Time' and if this attitude, which I'm sure it was, was echoed in his day to day work at the club and I'm not surprised that every manager that has ever worked with Jamie is quick to praise his professionalism as much as his ability on the field.

I feel this professionalism was further underlined in this season's 5-0 home victory over Swansea, when the game was at 4-0 I saw from my seat in the Paddock that when we won our second penalty Stevie G offered it to Carra. Now Carragher is no stranger to penalties as he's shown in previous shoot-outs but he is far from a regular taker and whilst he has never been quoted on his reasons for rejecting the offer I believe he didn't want to humiliate a Swansea team by a centre half with 5 goals in 700 plus appearances stepping forward just because the game was well won. After the game I tweeted what I saw which was well received and retweeted many times and what I saw was confirmed in a post-match interview with Gerrard.

Rafa trusted Jamie like he would trust a son, he was his rock at the heart of the defence and more recently Brendan Rogers realised the merits of having a Jamie Carragher in your starting line-up; even a 35 year old Carragher who is retiring at the end of the season. Liverpool now need not just a new centre back but another leader to fill the colossus void that Carra leaves behind.

Istanbul

by John Ritchie

25th May, 2005 -- There's been so much said and written about that night...

Liverpool fans looked on in despair as their team fell three goals behind to an AC Milan side who put on a master class in how the beautiful game can be played; Carlo Ancelotti's side, featuring Maldini, Cafu, Kaka, Gattuso, Seedorf, Pirlo, Crespo and Schevchenko, seemingly winning the Final inside the first 45 minutes and therefore fulfilling their tag as the best club side in Europe.

Back at home you could be forgiven for frantically looking on the internet to see what the biggest defeat was of any Final in the most famous club competition in the world. Most fans would have simply taken a 3-0 defeat at half time so as to spare them from further humiliation.

The fact Liverpool were even in the final in the first place was nothing short of a miracle. Nobody will forget the amazing intervention of Neil Mellor coming on to grab a goal and the assist for Steven Gerrard for the goal which became folklore and saw the Reds beat Olympiakos 3-1 at Anfield. On 75 minutes Liverpool were going out of the Champions League, by full time the Red's had completed another amazing European comeback.

Jamie Carragher was rightly hailed for his performances that season. His appearances alone showed the faith Rafa Benitez had in the boy from Bootle.

Who can forget his amazing performance in Turin alongside Sami Hyypia. Carra actually commented after the game that even though the Red' had done a job that night, Benitez didn't congratulate the team instead he criticised him for his movement on the ball and how he was slow in possession.

For some players that type of feedback after a top European performance may have destroyed confidence, but not Carra. He went on to deliver yet more stunning performances.

Carra's moment to shine was in the semi-final against Chelsea. Alan Hansen said after the two matches "his [Carragher's] performances defied belief. The way he held Chelsea at bay was unbelievable. I'm sitting there in awe of how many times he intercepted, blocked and covered."

That's high praise from Hansen who won 24 titles in his career at Liverpool. A man whose standards are known to be of the highest order; Hansen even said that Carra was better than him. Never known for his technical ability Carra's work rate, passion, commitment and leadership was the thing that always set him apart, something that Hansen said would see Carragher sit amongst the greats of an illustrious history at Liverpool.

Carragher showed everything he'd learned up until that point in his career; he read the game and did something we've all kind of got used to; he put his body on the line. Bravery is one of the hallmarks of his game, not just in tackling but also playing through excruciating pain.

Evidence of that if any was ever needed was demonstrated in extra-time of the final in Istanbul.

Many say that Liverpool never really won the final, that AC Milan threw it away. It's a possible argument, however looking back now the only player to really seem lost in the second half was Seedorf, he controlled the game so well in the first 45 minutes, but seemed baffled at what was happening in the second. He simply couldn't adapt to Liverpool's change in formation.

The argument Milan lost the final, is one that simply doesn't take into account something you can't train or coach into a player; character, aggression, determination and passion.

AC Milan had completely dominated Liverpool in the first half; the decision to leave out Didi Hamman left the side woefully exposed in midfield and with the truly world class team AC Milan had at the time, any defence would have struggled.

In that kind of situation even top class defenders struggle; when teams come under pressure, it's good to have an experienced head in your midfield to calm everything down and to try and control the possession in order to give the team a breather and try and stop momentum building up from the opposing side. But Liverpool's relatively youthful line up didn't quite have that mindset and Milan blew them away.

Many pundits afterwards criticised Carragher's first half performance saying he was strangely out of form. Yet Hamman has said repeatedly in interviews that AC Milan in that first half played the best football he'd ever seen.

What happened was that Liverpool had come up against some of the best technically gifted footballers in the game; a lot of people would class that as being better than Liverpool, however you're only better if you beat what's in front of you and AC Milan couldn't quite do that.

With that in mind Carra could have easily panicked at half time, he's said often that he just didn't want to be embarrassed; the manager didn't say anything inspirational, he was calm, made his decision to put Didi on and the rest of the squad just sat there kind of deflated.

Carra said "the thought of going home a laughing stock disturbed me; it would have felt like the whole city, the whole country and the whole world was taking the mickey out of us."

The fact that nothing inspirational was said; no epic team talk worthy of a Hollywood blockbuster movie, or a roaring speech with Rafa on a box like Al Pacino in 'Any Given Sunday', makes the comeback even more remarkable. Carra said all that Benitez did was quickly explain his tactics, diffuse the argument between

Steve Finnan and the physio and explain they were moving to a 3-5-2 in order to cut out Pirlo's influence in the game.

The confidence in the approach of what appeared to be an emotional Benitez at half time did something for Carra. He explained later that that the swiftness of the decision confirmed to him that Rafa had considered this earlier. It was the same strategy used in Turin, albeit it a defensive approach to the game. 'Ok' part of Carra was thinking 'Forty-five minutes too late, but we got there in the end'.

Carra revealed further that the rendition of You'll Never Walk Alone was un-like any he'd ever heard at Anfield, it was like a Hymn, the forty thousand Scousers in the Ataturk stadium, seemed like they were praying for the team. Carra reflected further "it was like the supporters way of saying 'we're still proud of what you've done, we're still with you, so don't let your heads drop". However Carra also felt there was another side to the message "don't let us down more than you already have."

The second half was as excited I think I've ever been as a Liverpool fan, it's also the most nervous, gut-wrenching and painstakingly end to end game of football as I've ever seen. When you think about the 'pressure' we felt as fans, you have to at one point give a thought for a player. These men are only human after all and to react in the way they did shows an element of the mindset required to play sport at the highest level.

To say Carra was responsible for the comeback would be an insult to Gerrard, Alonso, Smicer, Dudek, Hamman, Garcia and probably Carra himself; however there's no doubting Carra put his body on the line not just in physical effort. The repeated lines from Clive Tyldesley 'and it's Carragher again!!' summing it up referring to his sliding tackles, last gasp blocks that denying Crespo and Kaka in those scary moments.

I remember hearing the gasp when Carra slid in for an amazing challenge and lay there on the floor in agony with what looked like a groin strain. Liverpool had made all their substitutions by that point and I'm sure there wasn't one Liverpool fan either in the ground, outside in pubs and houses all over the world thinking 'Please no, not Carra'.

More breath-taking moments were to come, Dudek's double save against Shevchenko left many speechless; some commentators have said afterwards it was almost as if that was the moment when you knew that the Gods had deigned this was Liverpool's year. To this day, Dudek himself still doesn't know quite how he made those saves.

Despite the cramp, the obvious pain that most of the team were going through, the agony of Carra was clear for the world to see, the rest of the team made it through those final three minutes despite coming under severe pressure from Milan, with Crespo and Kaka causing all sorts of problems, Liverpool somehow managed to see it through to penalties.

Most professionals could be forgiven for thinking; well I'm not taking a penalty, that's me done for the night, but not Carra. His first reaction was to grab an already baffled Dudek and started screaming to "do it like Bruce"; Dudek commented after the game that he struggled to understand Carra at the best of times, but he could make out Grobbelaar and by the gestures Carra was demonstrating, he sort of understood that now was the time to try anything he could to distract the opposition, put them off.

The look on Carragher's face at the time typifies what we've seen of the man throughout his career, steely determination and passion, that red face of his dripped in sweat showing him to be, as many in the past have called him in the past and still to this day, a warrior.

Alas, the rest is history. Serginho and Pirlo missing Milan's first two penalties with Riise the only Liverpool player to miss that night. Dudek was to be the hero when he denied Shevchenko again, Liverpool were champions for the fifth time; a feat not repeated by any other English club.

In a game that showed both the sublime and the ridiculous of the beautiful game, Jamie Carragher demonstrated why we all love him. It was form he was to take into the next two seasons, being voted Liverpool's Player of the Year twice and cementing his place as one of the best defenders in Europe.

TLW Interview with Jamie Carragher

By Dave Usher, The Liverpool Way Fanzine (summer of 2005)

TLW: First of all, how does it feel to be a European Champion?

JC: Oh brilliant. We were all saying at the time that we didn't know when it would sink in, but I've been away for a few weeks and you get that many people coming up to you shaking your hand and congratulating you, so I think it's sunk in now. I saw a lot of footballers while I was away and they were all coming up saying congratulations and that. It's something I never thought would happen to me, and it's something I'll remember for the rest of my life. I've got it on video and I've watched it three times. I'll probably watch it again before we go back to training.

TLW: What was going through your mind in that first half though?

JC: When it was 1-0 we actually recovered quite well. We knocked it around well for the next five or ten minutes, so I was feeling alright then. Obviously you're sick you've conceded but I thought we were doing ok. Then they just kept picking us off on the break and Kaka was causing us a lot of problems. At half time I was just hoping it wouldn't be five or six. I didn't see any way back and I just didn't want any embarrassment for the club.

TLW: The second goal was a brilliant counter attack, but it should have been a pen to us for handball. Did you feel a bit cheated over that?

JC: Yeah the one with Luis. It was a Spanish referee, and when I heard that before the game I thought we might get a few favours, but he seemed to go the other way! It was a definite penalty, all this about did he mean to handball it.... handball is handball, it should have been a penalty. But that's just something that will be remembered as part of the game, and probably made our achievement even better.

TLW: What did Rafa say at half time?

JC: Everyone always asks me that, but what can you say when you're 3-0 down? There's not a lot you can say really. I think the big thing that happened was he had brought Djimi Traore off. Djimi had his boots off and was just about to get in the shower, when the physio said Finnan was injured. Finnan could have carried on because he'd had that injury before the game, but just out of the blue the manager said "No, we're changing. I'd have to take him (Finnan) off in twenty minutes anyway." So he brought Finnan off, Traore stayed on and we went to a 3-5-2. So the physio probably played a bigger part than the manager! If Finann had stayed on we were going to carry on with 4-4-2, with Riise left back and Garcia left midfield and Cisse coming on up front.

TLW: There were stories that the Milan players were celebrating on the way to the dressing room at half time. Did you hear any of that?

JC: No I never heard anything. I think the press jump on things and make a big deal out of them. I don't know if Djimi heard something, if he said he did then I'm sure he's not lying, but I certainly didn't hear it. We're talking about a top professional team, people like Maldini who I've got a lot of respect for. I can't see them doing that. Although I heard Gattuso was meant to be doing something when he came back out, gesturing to their fans or something?

TLW: The introduction of Hamann seemed to make a massive difference, as Kaka had been very influential in the first half. Were you surprised he didn't start the game?

JC: It was a big surprise to everyone. I don't think it was to do with who the manager brought in, I know a lot of people have mentioned about Harry Kewell starting, but I think it was more to do with us playing 4-4-2 instcad of 4-5-1 which we had been playing. We'd played that way all the way through with Stevie in an advanced role. So you just expect that manager is going to play that way for the final. That's the managers decision though, and I think the reason he did it was because when its two legs you can be a bit more defensive in one game, and that's what we did away from home. Against Milan I think he felt we had to go out and win the game, we can't sit back we have to be a bit bolder. It's something that Gerard Houllier was criticised for, but the manager has maybe gone the other way and people were criticising him for it. But it turned out well in the end.

TLW: The 2nd half has to be the greatest 45 minutes in the history of the club. Could you believe what was happening in front of you?

JC: When the third one went in I thought we'd win it in normal time. Riise then had a shot which the keeper saved, but then I think they obviously realised the situation and they came back stronger. I didn't even celebrate the first two goals because we were still getting beat. When the third one went in though I did!

TLW: You had a good view of the penalty incident didn't you?

JC: I saw Stevie running through and I knew something was going to happen. He was either going to get clipped or he was going to score. I was trying to get the wrong player sent off! I thought it was Nesta who clipped him and I was going to the referee to tell him to send him off. It was only when I watched the video I realised it was Gattuso who brought him down!

TLW: There were a lot of tired legs in extra time, and even you went down with cramp. It's often said that cramp is more painful than a broken leg. Do you agree with that?

JC: Yeah. The broken leg was very painful at the time, but it eases off. The cramp is really bad though. You just don't know what you can do to get rid of it. Every movement you make just seems to aggravate it. It's hard to explain to people who've never had cramp exactly what its like. I got it in the Carling Cup final as well, and its such a relief when it goes. This time I got it in my groin and I was thinking "I'm getting married in a couple of weeks and I've got cramp in my groin!" I was a bit worried about it but it eased off eventually.

TLW: What do you remember of Jerzy's double save?

JC: Well it was a great ball in. He saved the first one, but I was just waiting for the ball to hit the net. If it had we'd still have gotten credit for what we'd done, getting to the final and coming back from three down, but at the end of the day we'd have lost. It was one of them where you just can't believe it. I just can't believe how it stayed out. Credit to Jerzy, but it was a bad miss from Shevchenko.

TLW: Was that the moment when you thought we'd won it?

JC: Yeah I thought then we had a great chance, but having said that when the penalties kicked off and I saw the size of their goalie compared to Jerzy... fuckin ell... he was some size him wasn't he?

TLW: Why weren't you one of the five takers?

JC: I don't know. The manager said to me "Do you want to take one?" and I went 'yeah'. He was just going round asking people so I thought I must be taking one. I was one of the first people to say 'yes' but then he just said "this is the order we're going in" and I wasn't one of them. I don't think he's got much confidence in me, I'll have to show him the videos from the League Cup!

TLW: When you grabbed Jerzy and told him to do what Grobbelaar did, did you believe him when he said he knew all about it?

JC: I was really worried that Jerzy's too nice. He's a really nice fella, and I just thought he'd be stood in the goal being dead polite and nice. He's a top man, dead professional and all that, but whatever you wanna call it, gamesmanship, cheating or whatever.... fuck it.... he's got a European Cup winners medal now. I told him to do anything to put them off. He hadn't been booked, so kick the ball away and get booked, just do anything to gain an advantage. He is such a really nice fella that I was worried that he'd just be too nice in the goal. I just wanted him to try and do as much as he could to put them off, and he did.

TLW: When he made that winning save, all the players who were lined up on the halfway line sprinted to him. You beat them all by about ten yards, even Cisse. Does that make you the fastest man at the club now?

JC: *laughs* I've seen the picture where we're all taking off from the halfway line and I've got a bit of a start on them! I can't believe the reaction of some of the players. I knew he'd saved it and they're all just still stood watching!

TLW: When Lennart Johanssen mistakenly went to give you the trophy, you pointed at Stevie and told him to give it to him. Did you not just think 'fuck it I'm just gonna lift it"?

JC: Yeah I know! Obviously all the players would love to have lifted it, but with me being close to Stevie I know what it means to him being a local lad, and it's great for him. I know under Houllier we had different captains and people lifting it together and all that, but I know Stevie would never get involved in that type of thing. I think it's right that just the captain lifts it though. But on the actual moment he lifts it... have you seen the video of it?

TLW: Yeah you were somewhere away on the left....

JC: Well as he lifts it and everyone moves to the middle I got cramp again and was holding onto the barrier at the side. You can see it on the telly, it must have been that sprint to Jerzy that did it!

TLW: I read somewhere that you blacked out for a short time on the pitch, what happened there?

JC: No, that was bullshit. I fell on the floor, you know how when you're just overcome with emotion? I fell on the floor for a couple of seconds but that was it. Just the papers talking shite again.

TLW: You played in the UEFA Cup final against Alaves, which was one of the greatest European finals ever, but this one topped even that. Not bad for a team described by some as boring and defensive?

JC: Yeah, well both campaigns we probably got to the final because of our defensive strength. In the UEFA Cup we got to the final after keeping clean sheets in Roma and Barcelona, just like this time we kept clean sheets in Turin and at Chelsea. I think everyone just expected the final to be the same. I was talking with Stevie before the final and we agreed that the first goal would probably win it. So to lose a goal in under a minute, then lose two more but then end up coming back to win it shows what a great achievement it was. I think the Champions League needed a final like that, as a lot of the games are pretty boring and dead, so I think we've given a bit of life to the Champions League. It's just great that we've been in two of the greatest European finals of all time.

TLW: What did you do when you got back to the hotel?

JC: We had a party upstairs, but I couldn't enjoy it because I was getting so many people in. I must have got about 40 people in there! My dad and all that were in the hotel, but my brothers and them were outside so I was having to get them in. After that every ten minutes I was going back down trying to get people in, making up lies and saying they were my brother or uncles. Some fella actually got in the party saying he was my brother. Someone said "is he your brother" and when I said 'no' they threw him out!

TLW: Were you aware of how many banners there were with your name on? Did you see them in the stadium?

JC: No, they were a bit far away with the running track and that. We could see there were loads of them, but it was hard to see what they said. I've seen some of them in the club magazine, and it is great when you see things like that. The best one was the "For those watching in blue this is what a European Cup looks like"

TLW: Then of course there was the open top bus tour of the city. Were you surprised at how many people turned out?

JC: Me and Stevie and a few of the other lads were obviously involved in the treble one, but a lot of the lads couldn't believe what it was like when we got off the plane. I said to them "You've seen nothing yet" as I was expecting it to be like the treble one. But it surpassed that easily. The coach just couldn't move. At least in the treble one there were times when we could pick up a bit of speed but this time we were just crawling, that's why it took so long and it ruined our night out!

TLW: Proof of who the real people's club is?

JC: Yeah, I said that too. I got interviewed on the coach for the radio, and I said "Who's the people's club now?" That was something the Evertonians jumped on but its nonsense, both clubs have got a lot of support. We fill our ground every week and take thousands to Europe. We're the People's Club of the whole country! Look at the difference between the atmosphere in the game at Chelsea and the return at Anfield. People talk about the likes of Newcastle and Man City but when you see what our supporters did this season, and how they were in Turkey and the amount of people we took over there... we're the People's Club no doubt about it.

TLW: On the subject of Everton, are you aware of the daft rumours doing the rounds that you wear long sleeves because you've got an Everton tattoo?

JC: I know, but look. . . *rolls both sleeves up to reveal no tattoos at all*. . you can take a picture if you like! Someone even told me that it was a quiz question in a pub! I really don't know where it came from. I nearly always wear long sleeves, but I have worn short sleeves a few times. I get in the shower with the lads every day, so I'm sure it would have got out if it was true. There's that many rumours in Liverpool though, you know what its like.

TLW: I'm sure you also know about the rumour from last summer that you punched Gerrard when you were both with England. It was even printed a couple of papers. Obviously its not true, but have you spoken about it with him?

JC: Yeah, we actually went to the club to try and make a few quid from it, because they shouldn't write something like that when its total bollocks. Nothing ever come of it though. Obviously when I was away with England I was aware of what was going on, because I've got the same agent as Stevie. So I was aware that

Chelsea were interested and that, but that's up to himself. Obviously I've got my opinion and I'd love him to stay, I think he should stay and I think he will stay. It's better winning a Champions League with Liverpool than three or four with Chelsea or whoever else. If he'd have left last summer he wouldn't have a Champions League medal would he?

TLW: You have never been linked with any other club though.

JC: I know, none of the papers have ever linked me with anybody. I think it's because they all know I'd never leave.

TLW: Looking back at the road to the final, what did the players think in Germany when they found out Rafa had been down the boozer with the fans whilst you were all cooped up in the hotel?

JC: I just wish I'd have gone with him coz at least he got to see the game! We couldn't get any game in the hotel. I think Milan were playing Man United and Chelsea were playing Barcelona. We were all getting text messages from our mates and we could hear people screaming in the corridors when Crespo scored for Milan, so we knew United were out. Then there was the Barcelona comeback, so we thought Chelsea were going out too but then John Terry scored late on so we were all sick. I think the manager just went out to see the game, but obviously the fans love that because you don't want a manager who's too aloof, you want him to be one of the lads.

TLW: Obviously the games with Juve and Chelsea stand out. What was it like playing in those atmospheres?

JC: Oh it was unbelievable, especially the end of the Chelsea game. The supporters were all throwing the scarves round, it was just like they do abroad. You see it in South America with Boca juniors and that, and it was unbelievable. The Juventus game as well with the noise in the first half when we were scoring them goals, it was amazing. I know we're talking about moving to a new stadium and that, but I think we've also got to keep in mind that we don't want to lose that something special that we've got. It definitely puts fear into teams on European nights.

TLW: Exactly how much of an effect do you think it had on the opposition?

JC: A massive effect, no doubt about it. It has an effect on them, and it has an effect on us. I think with new stadiums the fans have to be so far away from the pitch, and there's no doubt that we'd definitely lose some of the atmosphere. You look at some of the teams who play in fancy new grounds. Derby were a decent team when they had the Baseball Ground, which was a tough place to go. Portsmouth now is a real tough place to go, but imagine if they get a new ground with a nice new pitch, it'd be totally different. It's not up to me to dictate what the club should do but for me we shouldn't lose what we've got. I'd prefer to stay. When it was first mentioned I liked the idea of a fancy new stadium, but the more I've thought about it.... I like the way the fans are so close to the pitch at Anfield. I follow European football closely, and whenever players are asked what their favourite English stadium is they always say Anfield. Obviously the Main Stand needs doing, and maybe that's the answer?

TLW: Of course it helps now that you don't get any stick from those fans close to the pitch anymore! No wonder you were in favour of a new ground a few years ago!

JC: I know yeah *laughs*...the cheeky bastards!

TLW: Were all the lads furious about what happened to Xabi in the 1st leg?

JC: I was more furious with him because I told him not to go so far forward and let Gudjohnsen run at us! It wasn't really even a foul, it was nothing. But when you come from behind like that. . . it was a bit like the Stevie penalty in the final. You know there's gonna be a tangle of legs, but to miss him for the second leg..... I mean he's as good as any, he'd walk into the Chelsea team for me. With his passing ability, especially at home, he was going to be a big loss. Fortunately we got through. I saw all the stuff in the press about what Gudjohnsen was meant to have said to Xabi, but I've always found him a decent fella when I've spoke to him. I don't know how true it was, but if he has said that then its out of order and it's probably came back to haunt him in the last minute at Anfield.

TLW: Were you worried about picking up a yellow card in the 2nd leg, or did you put it completely out of your mind.

JC: You say to people before the game that you will just put it out of your mind, but really I couldn't stop thinking about it. If you get the yellow card you've just got to keep going for the team of course, but you don't want to get booked for something stupid. It was always in my mind not to dive in and do anything stupid. I don't normally get booked that often to be honest so it's not something I was THAT worried about.

TLW: Do you think the Chelsea game was your best ever performance?

JC: Oh yeah definitely. With the magnitude of the game and with it being a European Cup semi final, to keep a clean sheet against them was a great achievement. They threw Huth up front, and you know the size of him. There was Drogba as well and they brought Robben on too, so for us to keep them out.... we did great.

TLW: What did Mourinho say to you after the game?

JC: I dunno, did he stop and speak to me?

TLW: Well there was a photo of him walking towards you, so I presume he did.

JC: I think he just came over and shook my hand, but he does that all the time trying to make out what a nice fella he is by coming on the pitch at the end. Then he goes off and says stupid things to the press after the game like: 'the best team lost'.

TLW: What did you make of those comments?

JC: They had a couple of chances at Stamford Bridge and maybe a couple at Anfield. Over the two games we had more chances and deserved to win. It's definitely sour grapes from him and I think he should have showed more respect for our manager.

TLW: You had a bit of a disagreement with him in Cardiff. What that was about?

JC: He had a go at Garcia for diving, yet he'd just come from fuckin Porto who had people like Deco who were never off the floor!! I've watched the Carling Cup final again, and Joe Cole does a couple of dives that nearly got Sami a booking. One of them might even have been the free kick that led to Stevie's own goal, I'm not too sure. John Terry dived trying to get a penalty in the final as well, and then you look at Carvalho dragging the keeper out the way for Terry's goal against Barcelona, and loads of other things. Yet here he is complaining about Garcia. So I told him to 'fuck off' and he started having a go. At the end of the game he came up to me and said "You know why I did that don't you?" basically trying to say that he was trying to influence the referee. But you know, whatever. . .

TLW: Was that the most painful defeat of your career?

JC: Yeah, because it was them. I don't think they are anyone's favourites here are they, and we were that close to winning and it was such a freak goal.

TLW: How do you explain a team that can win the Champions League, finishing 5th, below Everton?

JC: I don't know. But then a better Liverpool team than us did that in '81 as well. I'm not criticising anyone but I just think we've got to show more fight in the Premier league away from home.

TLW: I don't think there is anyone who would disagree that you were the clubs player of the season, but not counting yourself, who would you give it to?

JC: I thought Finnan played well. Early in the season it looked like he was going, I spoke to him and there was a chance he was going to move. He started the season at right midfield and played a few games there, although that wasn't his position. Then he got a chance with Josemi getting an injury and he come in and was superb. There was a bit of a question mark after his first season but to be fair he had a lot of injuries and didn't get a good run of games to show what he could do. This season though he was superb.

TLW: Players like Traore and Biscan really made an impression this season, and Igor managed to restore his battered reputation in his last season.

JC: Yeah after the La Coruna game I spoke to Stevie and said "you might not get back in." If Stevie had put in a performance like that everyone would have been raving about it. He put in a great performance, and made a great run for the goal. He also put a great pass through for Garcia against Leverkusen, and he played well against Juventus as well. I think it was unfortunate that he'd been here a long time but never really got himself settled. He was played out of position under the last manager, and I don't think that helped him too much. But he's shown that on the day he has got that ability it was a case of trying to get it out of him a bit more.

TLW: As you know, Igor is a bit of a cult hero in TLW. Do you have any funny Igor stories you can share with us?

JC: The funniest Igor story I've got is that I've never had a proper conversation with the lad in five years! Seriously, I've never had a conversation with Igor. Not that he's a bad lad, he's just very hard to get to know. He just comes in trains and goes home, he doesn't seem to speak to anyone really. We know he's a bit of a nutter in his car, and he was always laughing his head off on the phone when we were on the bus. It must be his mates who he's having a laugh and joke with, because he never did that with us. But he was always screaming on the bus laughing into his phone. We all used to sit there laughing our heads off because we'd never heard him laugh before.

TLW: Vladi has left now as well, but he went out with a bang with his goal and penalty in Turkey. You must have been pleased for him as he's a popular fella isn't he?

JC: Everyone is delighted for him, he was always laughing and joking on the training ground and he was always on the bus with his porno mags. They love it them Czechs, the two of them are dirty bastards! But he's a great lad and everyone is made up for him. I read an interview with him before the final where he said he didn't think the fans had really took to him, and to be honest when I read it I felt sorry for him because he's such a nice lad and to come out and say that about yourself shows his modesty. He was worried about actually being involved in the final, because he didn't make the squad for the Villa game. But his last kick for Liverpool was a goal, which is a great way to go out. If he ever comes back to Melwood he'll be welcomed back with open arms, as he really is one of the nicest fellas we've had at the club. It's unusual for a foreign player to have that sort of character.

TLW: Didi is staying though, I guess you're happy about that?

58

JC: Yeah, along with Stevie he's probably my best mate at the club, he's a great lad. I always think of some of the foreign lads as being a bit dopey when you talk to them, you know. Not that they're thick or anything, but being foreign they're not on the same wavelength, especially with the humour and that. But I've never met a fella so clued up as Didi. He doesn't just know English, he knows the slang as well. We can talk to eachother in our little scouse language and no-one else knows what we're talking about! It's brilliant how clued up he is, and I think people in town know he likes a pint and is a bit of a lad. But he always brings his 'A game' to the big matches.

TLW: Is it true that he turned down Everton this summer?

JC: Yeah he said he'd never go there because it would ruin everything he'd done at Liverpool, and I think that's right. He's had such a good career at Liverpool that he wouldn't want to tarnish that.

TLW: If Baros leaves, would you like the number 5 shirt?

JC: No, no. There's too many banners with 23 Carra Gold on them, so I'll be sticking with 23.

TLW: You and the rest of the lads must be sick of answering questions about Steven Gerrard, so I'm not going to ask any..... except are you sick of answering questions about Steven Gerrard?

JC: Yeah, of course and I've told him too. After the Juventus game all we were getting asked about was Steven Gerrard. We'd just beaten one of the best teams in the world and all we're getting asked about is him. That's not his fault though, that's the London press for you.

TLW: You've become a bit of a media darling recently, it seems everyone is saying nice things about you. Does that seem weird?

JC: Yeah it does. I think it's probably to do with me and Stevie being the only two English players here. Michael's gone, and he always had a bit of limelight. Obviously I think my performances have had something to do with it, but when we're playing in Europe and we come out to do the press afterwards, there's only me and Stevie who are English so I think the London press probably only know us. They only watch us a few times a season and probably don't even know who some of the other lads are! Maybe with me speaking to them it's doing them a favour so they write nicer things about how I'm playing. It has been nice, of course it has but I think it's basically a combination of my performances and Michael leaving which has put the attention onto others.

TLW: You even made the top three of the sports writers awards. Does that prove that the writers know more about the game than the players do?

JC: Yeah it probably does! Mind you, I think Lampard and Terry got about 95% of the votes. It was probably only Joycey (Paul Joyce from the Express) and Bascombe (the Echo) who voted for me, but it was enough to get me third place!

TLW: Alan Hansen said recently that you are ten times the defender he ever was. That's perhaps the biggest compliment a Liverpool defender could receive.

JC: Obviously I was delighted to hear comments like that from a fella like him. I think the key word though was 'defender', he didn't say 'player'!! He was a great footballer, probably the best centre back that Liverpool have ever had. I think what he meant by defender was that I'm a bit more aggressive than him, and put more tackles in than him. Obviously I'm delighted to have someone like Alan Hansen saying that, but I'm nowhere near as good as what he was.

TLW: What did you make of UEFA's decision. Should the FA have just sent Everton into the UEFA Cup?

JC: It would have certainly made it sweeter wouldn't it! Imagine that, if we'd knocked them out! I bet they were all delighted at half time, so imagine how delighted they would have been if they thought they were going to go into the Champions League, only for it to turn around in the second half. It would have been great, but we could still get them in the third round of the qualifiers. It's probably what UEFA want so they can get back to just four English teams. If it happens it happens, and to be honest I wouldn't mind because I think it'd be something to look back on and remember. It'd be two great games and great occasions, but there'd probably be a bit of trouble like!

TLW: There's been talk of the club pulling out of the world club championships. What's your view on that?

JC: I'd love to play in it. As soon as we won the final I was thinking about it for the next couple of days. No Liverpool team have ever won it, and to play against South American opposition like Boca Juniors or someone like that might never come round again in your career. It'd be good to see what they're like, with their different tactics and style of playing. It'd be a good challenge. It's a great accolade to win the World Club Championship, but if its not right for the club to do it and there's too many games then we have to do what's right, as the Premier League and the Champions League are more important. It's certainly something I'd love to have on the CV if we could win it though.

TLW: You've got a pretty sizeable medal collection now. Just one more to go for the full set. And yet you were asked by a reporter last season if you'd consider joining a 'bigger' club.

JC: Yeah, people talk about Chelsea and that but they've only won one Premier League title and the Carling Cup. Lampard and Terry are great players, but that's all they've won. Look at what we've won in the last four years. There's only the one left to win now, although I'd like to win some of the others again. We get criticised for not being successful, mainly because of how successful this club has been, but we shouldn't forget that since the turn of the Millennium we've won three European trophies. Look at the great Arsenal teams, they've never won a European trophy, yet we've won the Super Cup, UEFA Cup and Champions League, and we could win the Super Cup again.

TLW: Have you spoken to Robbie Fowler since the final, and if so is he planning on giving it the five finger salute at Old Trafford next year?

Yeah I've spoken to him a couple of times. He went over to the final with Macca, that shows what a great lad he is going over to watch the game with the supporters. I've seen him since and we've been out for a couple of drinks. He'll be changing it to five next season and giving them a bit of stick, and the season after hopefully he'll be able to give them six!

TLW: What do you think of the 'Team of Carraghers' song?

JC: I heard it for the first time in Leverkusen. Obviously it's nice to get things like that, with the supporters making up songs about you. I went for a few drinks after we won the Champions League and in a few pubs they were singing that, so yeah it's really nice to have the fans making up songs like that.

TLW: What's your favourite other song/chant?

JC: We've got a mate, Tony Hall, who knows them all word for word. And Bobby Wilcox as well, they always sing a 'Liverbird Upon My Chest' when we go out for a few drinks, and I think that's my favourite. And 'Ring of Fire' of course! [Carra senior nods in agreement.]

TLW: Finally, the last time you did an interview with us, we spoke about how you were sometimes the first one to get it in the neck from some sections of the crowd when things weren't going well. Now you're the most popular player at the club. Have you noticed any change in how you're perceived?

JC: Yeah, I think my performances have probably helped, but I always thought I was doing a good job before. I think maybe there were more star names there before, people like Michael and Robbie, who the crowd would look to. I suppose my performances have gone to a new level this season which has probably helped, and me and Stevie are the only two local lads. And also, there's no getting away from the fact that the Chelsea stuff with Stevie has probably took a little bit of attention away from him. Some of Stevie's biggest fans have probably become mine because I said I'd never leave and obviously that type of stuff helps with the supporters. But it's always been the way that the local lad often gets the most stick. I was an Everton fan as a kid and the first person to get the stick was John Ebbrell, even though he did exactly the same job as Barry Horne and Joe Parkinson. It was the same with Nicky Butt at Manchester United. It's just always been like that, Sammy Lee got a little bit of stick when he was a player didn't he. I think its just the easy option for the fans, as they're not gonna get on the back of someone who cost a lot of money. Although you could argue Harry Kewell maybe.

This interview is from the "European Champions Special Issue" of The Liverpool Way fanzine, printed in the summer of 2005. Visit www.liverpoolway.co.uk for details of how you can purchase the limited edition fanzine.

Retirement - What next?

by Dan Holland

When Jamie Carragher begins his extremely well earned retirement from playing football, what will he do with his time? After 16 years as a professional footballer it will surely be hard for him to switch off from a daily routine of training and matches once or twice a week. But how will Carra channel his energy?

For players who have played the game since the onset of the Premier League, invariably finance is not an issue and I envisage a number of players who are now reaching retirement retreating to their ivory towers and counting their wealth. There are obviously a number of players who you can tell eat sleep and breath the game and will stay involved at some level, surely Carragher is one of those.

In late April 2013 it was confirmed Jamie will be joining the Sky Sports panel alongside former Reds Jamie Redknapp and Graeme Souness as well as Gary Neville. Personally, I would be extremely disappointed if this was the only way that he stayed in the game in either the immediate or long term future.

When Kenny Dalglish re-joined Liverpool as manager and required an assistant I hoped that this would be the return of Liverpools 'boot room' culture and see Jamie become player/assistant manager. Then when the 'King' stepped aside, Carra would be the next manager with maybe Gerrard then making the step up and history repeating itself.

Liverpool legend John Aldridge shares a similar view, "From a selfish point of view as a Liverpool fan, I would love to see him stay around at Melwood. With so many youngsters coming through the club now, who better to have around them than Steven Gerrard and Jamie Carragher? There are no better players to show the new lads 'The Liverpool Way'. He's a great role model for the younger players and Jamie would be able to teach the new lads what the Premier League is all about. I would like him to stay at the club in the way they used to under Bill Shankly. If there is not a coaching role available then, at the very least, he could become an ambassador for the club."

These hopes were obviously allayed when Steve Clarke joined as Kenny's assistant, then when Brendan Rodgers was named our new manager I again hoped that he would want a 'Liverpool Person' in the ranks and again thought Jamie would be the man – disappointed again. An interview with Chris Bascombe in May 2013 revealed that "A discussion about joining Brendan Rodgers' backroom staff was cut short last summer, Carragher instead focusing on his final season as a player." While, "Sir Trevor Brooking's request for Carragher to join the England Under-20s World Cup coaching team was declined, the need for a clean break from the game taking precedence."

It seems as though becoming a coach or manager has at least crossed Carragher's mind and he has recently started his coaching badges. The FA appear keen to lead ex-pro's into management with Phil Neville and Owen Hargreaves also being mentored by the FA.

As well as being highly regarded as a footballer some well-educated scholars of the game anticipate Jamie having a successful future as a coach. "Having worked with Jamie Carragher it was always evident that he was a model professional who gave everything he had for club and country," says Roy Hodgson, the England manager. "After retirement I am sure he will march quickly up the coaching ladder and become one of the country's top young coaches."

Record appearance holder for the Reds, Ian Callaghan, has been quoted as saying "He [Carragher] is football mad and apart from being a great player, he is a top man for stats on the game. He is an intelligent guy. He has that mentality you need to be a manager."

The last Liverpool player I thought shared similar attributes to those that Carragher has in abundance and also talks lots of sense on the TV - or used to until years out of the game at times make his views seem somewhat outdated - is Alan Hansen. When Graeme Souness was sacked in 1994 rumours were rife at that point that Hansen may be the next manager, until he ruled himself out of the job. In an interview earlier this year Hansen answered the question quite unequivocally when asked if he ever considered management, he was quoted as saying "No, no, never. Management was never something I was interested in,"

Hansen has obviously enjoyed a successful career in broadcasting and kept his involvement in football this way, but to me it was a waste of a football brain that was so evident on the field. As I've already said I would be extremely disappointed if Carragher did 'a Hansen'. If, however, he follows the Gary Neville example [he says through gritted teeth and reaches for the mouthwash] it may be a good start to the post-playing career. Neville has become a very accomplished pundit and has slowly shed his Manchester United colours and become impartial never more in evidence than recently over the Luis Suarez 'bitegate'. He has mixed his TV career with a role as first team coach for the England National Team and seems a key part of Roy Hodgson's set up.

If Carragher were to become a member of Brendan Rodgers off field team at the same time as appearing on Sky Sports you can only imagine it would be in a youth role otherwise an obvious bias would be apparent not to mention a clash of diaries which would inhibit his TV role. This realistically only leaves a role with the national team as a coach in some capacity, this would be a shame as we would lose him from our great club. It would however give him invaluable experience on the other side of the white line that could then be used to all our advantages at Melwood and Anfield.

For now though, it seems Carragher will take a break, saying "If you'd asked me at the start of my career I would have said I was going to be a manager. I may still be in future. I always thought just because I love football, it doesn't necessarily mean I'm desperate to manage."

Whether TV or coaching is the ultimate destination for Jamie I'm sure you will all join me in wishing him all the very best for the future and we look forward to seeing you back at Anfield on many more occasions. My ultimate dream would be to see Carra lift the Premier League trophy as a manger that eluded him as a player, were it to be the one that put us back in front of United on titles won then that would be all the sweeter. Thanks for the memories Jamie lad and all the very best for you, your foundation and your family.

Liverpool's Top 10 Centre Backs

by Matt Sproston

You would be forgiven for thinking that over the last 50 years when Liverpool have been English football's most decorated club, that success would have been built upon a multitude of top quality centre backs. You would be wrong. The magnificent achievements of the club through the 60s, 70s and 80s were based upon the longevity of a handful of wonderful defenders. The fallow years since the last league title have seen a number of centre backs come and go with varying degrees of success.

Having said that, in order to make the top ten list you would have to be a seriously good footballer and to be in the top five you would have to be a club legend.

When compiling the list the following factors were taken into account: appearances; ranking within the "100 players who shook the Kop" fan vote; honours achieved; the writer's subjective opinion. Ultimately it is an opinion as appearances don't always mean trophies and many of the players in the list played in various positions through their Liverpool careers.

The list is drawn from players from the last 50 years. Undoubtedly there were players from the earlier history of the club that deserve mention but the centre-half or centre-back role as we now know it really only came into existence in the mid 1960's as teams changed from full backs and half backs to a back four.

In my opinion, the top eight pick themselves although the order is open for debate. Nine and ten are more difficult with some very good players just missing out. Gary Gillespie and Glenn Hysen were both terrific centre backs with league winners medals in their trophy cabinets. Stephane Henchoz was a stalwart of the success of Gerard Houllier's treble team. Steve Nicol was one of Liverpool's best ever defenders but only an occasional centre back. Likewise, Marcus Babbel was a wonderful footballer and a centre back for Bayern Munich and Germany. Had he remained fit and healthy he would certainly have moved inside from right back. All miss out on the list.

Ten - Daniel Agger – 209 appearances

A classy, ball-playing centre half whose Liverpool career has been blighted by injuries. Agger scored the semi-final goal that helped take the Reds to the Champions League final in 2007. Comfortable on the ball and strong in the tackle with good positional sense. He committed himself to the Reds in 2012 when a big money move to Man City was rumoured. He went on to have a largely injury free season with careful management and although the occasional goal has been conceded through marking errors at set pieces, he has been one of the Reds' outstanding performers under Rodgers.

Nine - Larry Lloyd – 218 appearances

The man whose middle name was "Valentine" was anything but a soft touch. Brought in by Shankly to ultimately replace Ron Yeats, Lloyd had the same commanding presence and strength. The team was in a state of transition when Lloyd made his debut in 1969 but it wasn't long before they were challenging for trophies and narrowly missed out on both the FA Cup and league titles. Lloyd was an ever present in the team that won the title and the UEFA Cup in 1973 and indeed scored in the UEFA Cup final. The emergence of Phil Thompson limited Lloyd's appearances and he left Anfield for Coventry City in August 1974. Lloyd went on to sign for Nottingham Forest and was a member of their European Cup winning teams.

Eight – Sami Hyypia – 464 appearances

If there was a top ten list of value for money signings, Hyypia would be right at the top. Bought for the sum of £2.5million, Sami was an unknown quantity when he arrived in Gerard Houllier's first transfer window as sole manager. He quickly established himself as one of the finest centre backs in world football. Magnificent in the air and strong in the tackle. He was a key member of the Houllier treble team and the Champions League winning team under Benitez. Popular with the fans and players alike, Sami never gave anything less than 100 percent for Liverpool. More trophies for the team would undoubtedly have seen him climb this list.

Seven – Mark Lawrenson – 356 appearances

Lawrenson became Liverpool's most expensive signing when he joined for a fee of £900,000 in the summer of 1981. He was a quick and skilful player and his ability saw him playing in midfield early in his Liverpool career. He also played full back before eventually settling into a partnership at centre back with Alan Hansen which is widely regarded as Liverpool's best defensive pairing. A succession of injuries blighted his career and forced him into early retirement. In only 356 appearances Lawrenson won 5 league titles and a host of cups including the European Cup of 1984. His perceived negativity towards Liverpool in his role in the media should not overshadow the fact that he was a top performer for the reds.

Six – Ron Yeats – 454 appearances

He may have had less ability than some and won fewer trophies than others on this list but Ron Yeats deserves his place on this list by virtue of being the foundation upon which Shankly rebuilt the club. Described by Bill as a "colossus", journalists were famously invited to walk around him. Yeats was tough as teak and a massive part of the team that gained promotion from the Second Division and went on to become First Division champions and FA Cup winners. Big Ron could do no wrong, even winning a European Cup quarter final on the toss of a coin. Ron was club captain for most of the 1960s and when he eventually lost his place to Larry Lloyd he acted with the dignity of a true gentleman.

Five - Tommy Smith – 638 appearances

As tough a player as there has ever been in a Liverpool shirt, Tommy was known as the Anfield Iron for good reason. Shanks said that Tommy wasn't born "he was quarried". However, he didn't make 638 appearances solely due to his ability to get stuck in. Tommy could play and had stints in midfield and full back. It was as a centre half that he is best remembered forging partnerships with Yeats, Lloyd, Hughes and Thompson that all brought silverware to Anfield. His powerful headed goal in the Rome 77 final was classic Tommy Smith and was the icing on the cake of a Liverpool career that earned him four league titles, a European Cup, two FA Cups and two UEFA cups.

Four – Phil Thompson – 477 appearances

Thommo is Liverpool through and through. A fan that stood on the Kop as a boy who eventually lifted the European Cup as captain. He also had a spell as caretaker manager when Gerard Houllier fell ill in 2001. He was tall and skinny when promoted from the youth team to the first team squad by Bill Shankly. Shanks reportedly beefed Thompson up with a diet of steak and chips. Despite his slender frame Thommo would never be found wanting for effort in a Liverpool shirt. Added to his desire was no small amount of technical ability and his ball playing skills were a key part of the club's philosophy of building from the back. An injury kept Phil out of the run in to the famous 1977 season but he still ended his Liverpool career with 2 European Cups and 7 league titles in addition to a host of other cups.

Three – Emlyn Hughes – 665 appearances

Two time European cup winning captain. England captain. Football Writers' Player of the Year in 1977. Hughes was plucked from lower league football by Shanks and became a Liverpool legend. His energy and enthusiasm allowed him to play anywhere in defence or midfield. His ability in bringing the ball out of defence allowed Liverpool to adopt a continental style of football which took them to four European trophies in 6 years. He also weighed in with more than his fair share of goals. His personality rubbed some up the wrong way and a high profile feud with

Tommy Smith has tainted his legacy. However, none of this should take away from the fact that Hughes was a seriously good footballer.

Two - Jamie Carragher – 737 appearances

Despite playing for Liverpool in their least successful period of the last 50 years, Carra ticks all the boxes. 7 major trophies won. Liverpool's second highest appearance maker and possibly could have carried on to challenge the record. Popular with the fans. Wholehearted. Passionate. He will be remembered for the mind boggling performance in Istanbul after half time but Carra would throw himself around like that whether he was playing Aldershot or AC Milan. Underrated technically but still good enough to play in midfield for England. A succession of Liverpool managers have been won over by his industry, ability and leadership. His organisational qualities, fine-tuned under Rafa, have proved invaluable and will be impossible to replace.

One – Alan Hansen – 620 appearances

Hansen's record makes it simply impossible to be sentimental and give the number one spot to Carra. 8 league titles, 3 European Cups, 2 FA Cups and 4 League Cups were won during his time at Anfield. Hansen was technically gifted and cool under pressure. He made the game look so easy. Very rarely was he caught out of position and his reading of the game meant he would nick the ball from opponents without the need to go to ground. Often this resulted in a counter attack with Hansen thinking nothing of carrying the ball from one end of the pitch to the other. His languid style was criminally overlooked by Scotland but it was certainly appreciated by the reds fans and he remains massively popular to this day.

Carragher - The Goals!

Goal 1- vs Aston Villa - 18 January 1997

Making his full debut at Anfield, Carragher lined up in central midfield alongside Jamie Redknapp after new signing Bjorn Tore Kvarme was cleared to play. Carra was booked inside 20 seconds! "That calmed me down" he joked after. His goal arrived shortly after half-time. Carragher lost his marker and headed in Stig Bjornebye's corner at the Kop End from 6 yards out into the bottom corner. Liverpool won the game 3-0, with Stan Collymore and Robbie Fowler adding the goals.

Goal 2 - vs Southampton - 16 January 1999

Carragher scored the fifth in a 7-1 rout of Southampton. Jamie Redknapp fired in a fierce 25-yard free-kick that ballooned up off the diving Saints keeper Paul Jones for Carragher to follow up and smash home. The game was memorable for a Robbie Fowler hat-trick that took him past the 100 League goals marker.

Goal 3 - vs FKB Kaunas - 26 July 2005

Carragher scored his first goal for more than 6 years in a Champions League qualifier in Lithuania. The match was just 2 months after the historic victory in Istanbul. Carragher headed home from a Gerrard corner in the 29th minute, with Djibril Cisse and Gerrard (pen) giving Benitez's side a 3-1 win in the first leg.

Goal 4 - vs Fulham - 9 December 2006

By now a regular in Rafa Benitez's defence, Carragher scored the second goal in a 4-0 win over Fulham. Steven Gerrard's corner at the Kop End was flicked on by Daniel Agger and Carragher slid in at the back post to stab home from close range. His first League goal for almost 8 years!

Goal 5 - vs Middlesbrough - 23 August 2009

This is the goal that was actually taken away from Carra by the Premier League's dubious goals panel, after his shot was deflected in off Middlesbrough defender Emanuel Pogatetz. However, Liverpool FC's stance is that the goal remains Carragher's.

Trailing 1-0 with five minutes remaining of the first home game of the season, Liverpool were pressing down the right side of the pitch when Xabi Alonso's blocked cross fell for Carra to pounce on just outside the box. His shot was driven towards the far post only for it to hit Pogatetz and deflect into the near side of Turnbull's goal at the Kop end. Steven Gerrard's goal in stoppage time capped the comeback - the same scoreline occurred in the next match too, defeating Man United after going behind early on.

... and the own goals!

	Opposition	Date	Comp	Score
1	Tottenham	5 Dec 1998	PL	L 2-1
2	Tottenham	1 May 1999	PL	2 3-2
3	Man United	11 Sep 1999	PL	L 3-2
4	Man United	11 Sep 1999	PL	L 3-2
5	West Ham	13 May 2006	FA Cup Final	D 3-3 (W on Pens)
6	Tottenham	1 Nov 2008	PL	L 2-1
7	Hull City	13 Dec 2008	PL	D 2-2
8	Blackburn	24 Oct 2010	PL	W 2-1

Carragher Quotes

"It has been a privilege and an honour to represent this great club for as long as I have and I am immensely proud to have done so and thankful for all the support I have had. There are many memories I want to share and people to thank, but now is not the time for that."

- on announcing his retirement

"I don't go on the websites or anything but I believe there's murder there after a game if we have got beaten. But I'm not kidding people, if the team were to get beaten then I know I'd be one of the first to get criticised!"

- Carra in 2003

"I knew the night before, I was down to play at centre-half but Bjorn Kvarme's clearance came through before 5pm that night but I didn't realise. I wouldn't have been playing only that Patrik Berger was sick that night, so there was a place and I was moved into midfield. I was a bit nervous, but it was more excitement really. I got booked after 20 seconds, that calmed me down."
- On his full debut against Aston Villa in 1997

"There's no point sulking about it. There's not a lot you can do, except impress the manager in training and in games. Or find out his (Finnan's) address and send the boys round!"

- Carra was asked by Sky Sports about the arrival of Steve Finnan

"There may be more skilful players in the squad, but no one can ever say I don't give 100%"

"When I say life, I mean it. I want to stay here. When I say that, it's not talk, I really mean it. I mean I'm not kidding myself, I don't think I'm going to go any higher than Liverpool. If your club's in the Champions League that's the ultimate and obviously you want to win trophies. "

"I've been lucky enough to do that here in the past and I want to win bigger trophies now, the Champions League and the Premiership. We're not at that level yet but the new manager, if he can bring in a few more players, can get us to that level. I've never even thought about leaving."

- Carra in March 2005

"When the news came through on the TV, I nearly choked on my cornflakes."

- Pleased at the news of Steven Gerrard's transfer U-turn

"For me, it was probably Eidur Gudjohnsen missing the chance in the final minute when we played Chelsea. For a second, my heart was in my mouth. I thought we had thrown everything away that we had worked so hard all season to achieve. When his shot whistled past the post, it was a signal that we were going to the final and, for me, it was the sign that we were going to do it."

- Asked to pick out one moment from the Champions League campaign

"I'll be on a bender for a week."

- Carragher after Istanbul

"I love playing games. I want to play as many games as I can. I'm not going to break any goalscoring records, so I'll just have to try to break a few appearance records."

"He thinks he's a bit of a star doesn't he? But he has one of the worst strike rates of any forward in Liverpool history. He's the only no. 9 ever to go through a whole season without scoring , in fact he's probably the only no. 9 of any club to do that. He was always the last one to get picked in training."

- Carragher is not a fan of El Hadji Diouf

"I think everyone just thinks he is a bit stupid now, I think he embarrasses himself, he's just like a big baby isn't he? He's a great manager in what he's done, but I don't think you can say he is a great man. There's nothing wrong with defending your players, or playing mind games, but Mourinho just takes it too far. He always seems to be talking about other teams and other players."

- Carra in April 2006 on Jose Mourinho

"Who's bigger than Liverpool? I'm not having that. I've already got four or five medals here and I'm sure I'm going to win some more".
- When asked by Geoff Shreeves if his performances could get him a move to a "bigger club" than Liverpool.

"People call me a 'classic scally'. I take that as a compliment."

Tributes to Carragher

"Carragher is 10 times a better defender than I could ever be. He is a completely different player. He is a great defender whereas I was not. My strengths were on the ball, positional sense and recovery pace. The way he held Chelsea at bay was unbelievable. I'm sitting there in awe of how many times he intercepted, blocked and covered. I think if we look at Liverpool greats over the years - and there have been a lot of them - Carragher is up there with the best of them."

- Alan Hansen in May 2005

"We have big names in our defence which is probably the best in Europe. Liverpool don't have that but they have players to be respected, especially Carragher who is now the third-best defender in the Premiership and has proved very impressive."

- Paolo Maldini in May 2005

"My room-mate on away trips is one of the genuine Scousers. He's full of funny digs and gives the foreigners some light-hearted stick. As a local lad he has hundreds of mates who are Liverpool fans and is always looking for tickets for them. Suddenly he becomes really friendly with the foreign stars because their need for tickets is not as great as his."

- Michael Owen in 2001 on Carra

"If you understand Carra, you'll understand everyone."

- Rafa to Fernando Morientes when he arrived at the club

"Although you've got a mix of German, Swiss and Finnish in the back four, we all speak to each other in English. The only problem, though, is that none of us can understand Jamie Carragher!"

- Stephane Henchoz

"I'm very close to Jamie, we're good friends. Jamie is more into football that anyone I know. He thinks Sky+ is the best invention ever. He tapes every single sports show and watches them continuously! He's obsessed!"

"Before the penalties, Carra came up to me like he was crazy - as always! He said: "Jerzy, Jerzy - remember Bruce (Grobbelaar). He did crazy things to put them off and you have to do the same".

"The best defender I've played with at Liverpool and the worst finisher I've ever played with!"

"For me Jamie is one of the best defenders in Europe. He is always focused on the game, always trying to learn. That is the key for me because each season he improves a little bit. He is always listening and that is one of the reasons he can keep improving. It is the same every training session, always working hard, always trying to improve. He reminds me of a hunting dog, when I want something specific done in defence he is very willing to learn. As a defender he is someone you do not want to play against, to have marking you.

He has a strong character. He is always shouting and talking to the others, such a key player for us. He is good for the young players, showing them what to do and how to play. Carra lets them know what is expected. It is so important, he puts people under pressure and that is really good for team spirit. Jamie is playing really well, for the last two seasons he has been a really key player for us."

On the announcement of his retirement:

"Sorry to hear the news on Carra, his quotes regarding retirement tell you everything about the man... An absolute legend of a player."
- *Robbie Fowler*

"What a servant Carra has been for Liverpool. A rare breed and it's been a privilege to play alongside, room with and be big mates with one of footballs real men. I doubt we have heard the last of him. He has too much to offer the game to be away for long!"
- *Michael Owen*

"Just read Carra statement. Let's enjoy a few more months with him before he retires. It is amazing what he is done for LFC. #23"
- *Lucas*

"Jamie Carragher has been a great servant to Lfc. Great player & a top fella! Funny guy! Nutter when we were kids but management material now."
- *Rio Ferdinand*

"Jamie Carragher will hang up his boots at the end of the season. Those boots were worn by a player respected by everyone in the game."
- *Gary Lineker*

"Sad day for Carra announcing his retirement. He'll be missed but he can be very proud of everything he's done for Liverpool."
-                          *Kenny   Dalglish*

Top 10 Carra Memories

As chosen by members of the This Is Anfield forums; words by Broomy.

1) The 1996 FA Youth Cup Win

"The adrenaline rush, the anxiety beforehand, as you want to do yourself justice, the yells of approval as you approach the climax; and the feeling that your sharing something special. That's what winning your first trophy does to you" words used by Carragher to describe his 1996 Youth Cup Final win. A week after the white Armani suits FA Cup Final, the Liverpool Youth Team faced West Ham over a two-legged Final, the club who had beaten the Reds in the Final more than 30 years earlier. Carragher began that season Youth Cup run as a relatively unknown 18 year old but ended it on the threshold of a senior debut. This was Liverpool's first ever youth Cup win, a team full of bright prospects such as David Thompson, Phil Brazier, Jon Newby, Michael Owen and Carragher. It may have been his first trophy for Liverpool but unknown to Carragher at the time it would be the first of many.

2) Liverpool Debut

A baby faced Carragher burst onto the Liverpool scene on January 8, 1997 against Middlesbrough in the League Cup Fifth Round.

With Liverpool trailing 2-1, Roy Evans gave Carragher his Liverpool first team debut in midfield fifteen minutes from time replacing Rob Jones as Liverpool went looking for the winner. But it was Middlesbrough who hung on to progress to the League Cup fourth Round. 28,670 supporters packed the stadium witnessing Juninho, Emerson and Fabrizio Ravanelli steal the show but unbeknown to them was a young 18 year old making his debut who would go on to join the true Liverpool greats - Ian Callaghan, Tommy Smith, Ray Clemence, Alan Hansen, Bruce Grobellar who have served 14 or more consecutive years with the club.

3) Debut goal against Aston Villa

On 18 January 1997 at home to Aston Villa, Jamie Carragher made his full Liverpool debut - a game which endeared himself to the Anfield faithful. Before the match Jamie had arrived at Anfield expecting to be playing at centre back. Bjorn Toure Kvarme had just signed from Rosenborg but his international clearance wasn't expected to be cleared on time but that morning Kvarme has given the green light to play.

Carragher was demoted to the bench but fortunately for Jamie, Patrik Berger fell ill giving Carra the chance to play in a midfield role alongside Jamie Redknapp. It was Kvarme who grabbed the man of the match award but it was the young 18 year old from Bootle who grabbed all the headlines.

Facing the experienced Andy Townsend, Carra was booked for a foul in the very first minute! But unfazed as ever, Carra never looked out of place, turning in a confident performance. He marked his full debut in fine style shortly after the interval when he drifted into the box to meet Stig Igne Bjornebye's corner, heading the ball into the goal at the Kop End, paving the way for a comfortable 3-0 victory!

4) The Birmingham Final

The first of the Treble - The 2001 Worthington Cup Final... Liverpool looked destined to claim their first trophy of the season when Robbie Fowler opened the scoring with a well taken volley on the half-hour mark but a late Darren Purse spot-kick took the match into extra-time and later, penalties. McAllister, Barmby, Ziege and Fowler scored for Liverpool, Pulse, Marcello, Hughes and Lazaridis all scored for Birmingham while Grainger and Hamman missed. Up next was Carragher who scored a neat right footed shot into the top corner, ultimately it was Sander Westerveld who was Liverpool's spot-kick hero as he saved from Andy Johnson to cap a dramatic encounter in The Millennium Stadium but Jamie scored the vital penalty for Liverpool in the shoot-out when he showed bottle and guts to secure his first Liverpool first team trophy.

5) The night of the Cup Treble

Jamie Carragher recently spoke on how these three winners medals represented the season when the players reserved their place in Anfield folklore. It was the treble that had never been achieved before by an English side... Carragher played the full 90 minutes plus extra time in which an own goal by Alaves defender Delfi Geli became Liverpool's golden goal amid scenes of mayhem in Dortmund. The anti-climax of the own goal failed to curb Liverpool's celebrations; a European trophy was on its way back to nestle inside the Anfield trophy cabinet for the first time in 17 years, and Carragher was part of it! Carragher was instrumental in helping the Reds to the Treble during the 2000/01 season having featured in 58 games of the 63.

6) The Broken Leg at Ewood

In September 2003, Carragher suffered a broken leg in a tackle with Blackburn Rovers full-back Lucas Neill. His grit and determination ensured before he was forced to leave the field with the injury, he made a decent fist of attempting to play on regardless - not realising how serious the injury was.

Speaking to The Guardian newspaper following the game, Carra described the moment: "I wasn't aware of it until the next morning. I slept on it that night; I wasn't quite sure what I'd done. It was painful but I'd visions of being back in a couple of weeks. The problem was our doctor had already gone to the hospital with Milan [Baros], so he couldn't look at me when I'd done my leg. The Blackburn doctor looked at me, but then as soon as our doctor looked at me on the Sunday morning, within 10, 20 seconds, he said, 'You better go to the hospital.' It was confirmed then."

7) Istanbul

Istanbul will always be the highlight of Jamie's Liverpool career. To win the Champions League is to reach the pinnacle of your profession for most footballers, and yet, at half-time it was looking like being the low point for Carragher. Those 30 minutes of extra time will be what Carragher will always be remembered for in years to come; courage, character, determination and above all his willpower as he battled cramp with an amazing performance to help Liverpool produce The Miracle in Istanbul.

Ubermick reminisces : "In terms of great Carra memories, it has to be Istanbul. His performance on the pitch despite his legs shutting down earlier in the match, followed by the brief history lesson he gave Dudek, followed by him losing the plot completely when Dudek saved Shevchenko's penalty and going off on his meandering sprint around the pitch."

Dane : "One of my everlasting memories of Carragher are from that night in Istanbul, where his attitude grit and determination overcame the severe cramp problems he was having, and he continued to throw his body around when lesser players would have limped off. Speaks volumes for the man."

Broomy : "Racing over to Dudek and recounting the tale of Bruce Grobbelaar in Rome 21 years earlier"

Sam Wanjere : "Istanbul where he was immense. I'll never forget the tag of "Marathon Man" bestowed him by Johan Cruyff. Anytime legends like Cruyff mention you, you're on Legend Boulevard!"

8) A giant among men

On 21 September 2007, Liverpool travelled to the Nou Camp for the first leg of the Champions League tie first knockout round. In the delicate facets of the game Liverpool came perilously close to being eviscerated by a Barcelona team - the reigning champions, who outplayed the Reds scoring in the thirteenth minute. Liverpool produced one of the most stunning results in their proud European history as they came from behind to defeat Barcelona 2-1, courtesy of goals by Craig Bellamy and John Arne Riise.

Carragher produced a magnificent performance showing a big heart and strong mind turning in a performance of a lifetime which doesn't come much better than Barcelona away. In the words of Alan Hansen: 'they've got arguably the best player in the World in terms of technical ability plus others with pace, fantastic ability and many other qualities but Carragher played like a giant among men'. Jamie was later voted man of the match playing against Ronaldiniho, Messi and Eto'o.

9) Chelsea at Anfield

Jamie has treated us to some truly inspirational performances over the years but the Chelsea semi final second leg in 2007 is legendary as Liverpool overturned Chelsea's first leg lead with an inspirational performance at Anfield.. Not only did Carragher produce one of his best performances in a Liverpool shirt he also set a new European club record of 90 games, eclipsing the great Ian Callaghan.

10) Testimonial

With every penny raised from his testimonial going to charities in the area via his 23 Foundation, it was a day for all Reds to indulge in nostalgia and celebrate Carragher's 15 seasons in the first team at Anfield. Over 35,682 supporters were at Anfield to watch the city's two top-flight teams lock horns in his richly-deserved testimonial. Carragher marked his testimonial with a goal for each side as Liverpool beat an Everton XI 4-1 at Anfield.

Player Profile

James Lee Duncan Carragher

Born: 28th January 1978; Bootle, Merseyside

Personal Honours: PFA Team of the Year (2006), Liverpool FC Player of the Year (2005, 2007), Freedom of the Metropolitan Borough of Sefton (2008), Honorary Fellowship from Liverpool John Moores University (2012).

Liverpool FC

Honours: FA Cup (2001, 2006), League Cup (2001, 2003, 2012), UEFA Cup (2001), Champions League (2005), Charity Shield (2001, 2006), European Super Cup (2001, 2005), FA Youth Cup (1996).

Appearances: 737
Goals: 5

Debut: vs Middlesbrough (a) 8th January 1997 - League Cup Fifth Round

Full debut: vs Aston Villa (h) 18th January 1997 - Premier League

First goal: vs Aston Villa (h) 18th January 1997 - Premier League

Last goal: vs Middlesbrough (h) 23rd August 2008 - Premier League

Last appearance: vs Queens Park Rangers (h) 19th May 2013 - Premier   League

International

Appearances: 38 (21 as sub)

Debut: vs Hungary (a) 28th April 1999 - Friendly
Last appearance: vs Algeria (n) 18th June 2010 - World Cup 2010 Group

Major tournaments: Euro 2004, World Cup 2006, 2010
Squads named in: 62

England Under 21s: 27 appearances

Appearance Data

Season	Appearances					
	League	FA Cup	League Cup	Europe *	Other **	Total
1996-97	2	0	1	0	0	3
1997-98	20	0	2	1	0	23
1998-99	34	2	2	6	0	44
1999-00	36	2	2	0	0	40
2000-01	34	6	6	12	0	58
2001-02	33	2	1	16	1	53
2002-03	35	3	5	11	0	54
2003-04	22	3	0	4	0	29
2004-05	38	0	3	15	0	56
2005-06	36	6	0	13	2	57
2006-07	35	1	1	13	1	51
2007-08	35	4	3	13	0	55
2008-09	38	3	1	12	0	54
2009-10	37	2	1	13	0	53
2010-11	28	0	0	10	0	38
2011-12	21	5	5	0	0	31
2012-13	24	1	2	11	0	38
Totals	508	40	35	150	4	737

* Europe = Champions League, Europa League. ** Other = World Club Cup, Charity/Community Shield, European Super Cup.

Credits

Photo credits:

Mandy Davis
Craig Hulland / CH Photography

Contributors:

Matt Ladson @mattladson
Max Munton @maxmunton
Matt Sproston @spros1
Dan Holland @danhollandlfc
John Ritchie @JohnRitchie84
Dave Usher @theliverpoolway
Gavin Cooney @gavincooney1982

This Is Anfield
www.thisisanfield.com

3701431R00053

Printed in Great Britain
by Amazon.co.uk, Ltd.,
Marston Gate.